A SAMPLER OF FORMS FOR SPECIAL LIBRARIES

Second Edition

Social Science Group
Washington, DC Chapter
Special Libraries Association

1700 Eighteenth Street, NW
Washington, DC 20009

Manufactured in the United States of America

ISBN 0-08-711356-2

Library of Congress Cataloging-in-Publication Data

A Sampler of forms for special libraries/Social Science Group, Washington, DC Chapter, Special Libraries Association. —2nd ed.

p. cm.

Includes bibliographical references and index.

ISBN 0-08-711356-2: $29.00

1. Libraries, Special —Forms— Handbooks, manuals, etc. 2. Library science—forms—Handbooks, manuals, etc. I. Special Libraries Association. Washington, DC Chapter. Social Science Group.

Z675.A2S25 1991

025.5'66—dc20 90-27762

CIP

CONTENTS

FOREWORD

This book is intended as a guide to help the librarian develop useful forms for the provision and measurement of library services. It has value not only for small or new libraries, but also for any librarian initiating a new activity or facing complex, error-prone, repetitive tasks, and who knows *there must be a better way.*

The *Sampler* has three parts:

1. A discussion of forms design, reprinted from *Forms Design and Control* by permission of the American Management Association, demonstrates how to design a form and gives a checklist of principles to observe. We include this chapter to give the reader an understanding of what a form ought to be.

2. The sample forms which comprise the main portion of the book were collected from libraries throughout the Washington, DC metropolitan area by members of the Social Science Group, Washington, DC Chapter of the Special Libraries Association. The forms were chosen for best exhibiting principles of good design, usefulness, and general applicability. Not every form rates highly in each area, but each is included because the editors feel it has something to offer. The forms have been modified to remove reference to the originators.

   Form letters are included in several sections. While not forms in the usual sense, such letters are used by many libraries, and they share the same purpose as other forms to assist in the efficient operation of the library.

3. The annotated bibliography provides a selective overview of literature about forms in libraries along with some references from business forms sources which we felt were relevant to the library setting.

First published in 1982, *A Sampler of Forms for Special Libraries* evolved out of an earlier project by the Social Science Group. A committee composed of Grace Waibel, Chairperson (US Bureau of the Census), Alice Neff (Brookings Institution), Dora Kellenson (AFL-CIO), Gene Kubal (US Army), and Mary Pike (National Association of Housing and Redevelopment Officials) collected forms, weeded them, and compiled a notebook which was informally circulated among librarians in the Washington area who needed suggestions on designing forms. The Group felt that the notebook was useful and that the materials merited a wider audience. A second committee, consisting of Pamela Tripp-Melby, Chairperson (ACTION), Joan Bow (Robert R. Nathan Associates), Olivia Kredel (National League of Cities), and Phil Pacheco (Hogan and Hartson), was formed to develop the notebook into publishable form. Both the first edition in 1982 and this, the second edition, depend heavily on the work of that first committee. Their valuable contributions are gratefully acknowledged.

The committee which undertook preparation of this revised edition consisted of Michael Kolakowski, Chairperson (Congressional Research Service, Library of Congress), Cherie Allen (Congressional Research Service, Library of Congress), Joan Bow (Robert R. Nathan Associates), William Neff (Smithsonian Institution), and Sommers Pierce (American Bankers Association). The annotated bibliography was compiled by Peggy Garvin (Congressional Research Service, Library of Congress).

Special thanks are due to the libraries that contributed the forms appearing in these pages. This compilation would not have been possible without their generosity and cooperation. The officers and members of the Washington, DC Chapter of SLA were unfailing in their enthusiastic support for the project.

A Sampler of Forms for Special Libraries, Second Edition, contains forms from libraries large and small, public and private, new as well as long-established. The forms were submitted by libraries in government agencies, law, medicine, media, arts, trade and professional associations, research and academic institutions. We in the Social Science Group and the entire Washington, DC Chapter of the Special Libraries Association are very proud of the wealth of special library resources in the Washington area, and we are pleased to offer this publication to our colleagues on their behalf.

MECHANICS OF FORMS DESIGN

You don't have to be an artist to produce a thoroughly useful form. Even if you can't type, print, or draw a straight line with a ruler, you can create a form that will do a job you can justly take pride in.

A form that is truly necessary will not duplicate information supplied or requested by any other form. It will be called upon, therefore, to give management certain details about operations or control over them. In this sense, a well-designed form that meets a real need is as much a company asset as is any other business property. For as long as the form is useful, perhaps permanently, it will provide its information to any person who may need it. If the form has been well made, its facts will be presented simply, completely, and effectively.

Some would-be forms artists sit at an easel and struggle with lettering devices, colored inks, drafting tools, and assorted apparatus. The better artists will, of course, produce more beautiful designs than those who have less experience with drafting techniques, but both the skilled and the unskilled will have wasted their time if the resulting forms are pretty rather than thoroughly useful.

If the designer must be deft of hand because the form created will be reproduced by a spirit duplicator, mimeograph machine, or similar process, the drafting of the form will be a critical process. In such cases, artistic endeavor pays off to some degree. But in today's business world, given the essential requirement for data control as well as the huge cost of clerical time, it hardly pays to tie up the time of anyone capable of preparing a genuinely valuable form by insisting on manual output. It will suffice, in the great majority of cases, if the designer indicates what is wanted on the form and where, then specifies what lines, type faces, and so on should be used. From that point, the printer should take over; the printer can bring back a professional-looking job which will do its work as well as the design permits.

When the boss says, "We could use a form to keep track of..." and you are assigned the job of creating it, there is no need to rush out for art materials or to don a painter's smock. Nor is there need to wince because drawing your breath is the only drawing ability you possess. Your first task, far from being an artistic one, is most mundane: You must immediately begin to assemble all—every bit—of the data that the form should have incorporated in it. You can't forget one scrap; should there be a significant omission, the form will have to be redone or will at best be only partly useful.

The first step is therefore to become thoroughly familiar with the project the form is intended to control or implement. You may find this information in the company's standard procedures—if there are any and if such instructions are actually up to date. But to rely on standard procedure alone is hardly enough; it would be wise to supplement whatever information you have at your desk in procedure manuals with whatever you can pick up along the path over which your record will ultimately travel. Questioning personnel who will handle it may provide otherwise unthought-of additions; at the very least they will show the sequence of stops on the route of record flow and so help you to position each item on the form.

To insure that all the components are included, you should prepare a list of points to be covered and check with all the prospective users to determine whether any items should be added and whether any can be eliminated. Be careful, though, to check before removing anything from the list of components; items that some people consider unnecessary may be urgently required by other users of the form.

As an example, one insurance company decided to make up a new questionnaire for policy applicants. The old form had certain details in its structure which all the departments that were consulted agreed were superfluous. But one department was not consulted—on the assumption that it had no connection with the form. The new questionnaire was designed without any of the "extraneous matter" in it; then, about a month later there was a storm of protest. The old form had to be brought back into use for that single department. Which, of course, is a violation of the rule that there should not be two forms where one will suffice.

It isn't always easy to determine who will use or refer to a form. Information about its flow and about the people who requisition it from supply is simple enough to check out, but sometimes one element escapes notice. And any deletion of required data or failure to include a pertinent topic can cause problems.

Once the list of components has been made up and found to include all the essentials, the layout or presentation of these items must be considered. The most important items, those that deserve top billing, should be placed at the top so that they are prominent. Basic is the form's title, for by its name people will recognize it, select it, use it. Next in importance is any modification of the title, for example, the words "Office Machines" following the heading "Requisition Data." The subtitle need not be in as large a type as the title, and this should be indicated for the printer's guidance.

The sequence of the items that follow these salient data should correspond with the form's flow. Our eyes are trained to read from left to right. Also, we see things better if they are arranged in block formation. It is wasteful of clerical time—a most expensive commodity—to make a form's users search for a portion of it they must complete or gather details from. If all items are presented in a left-to-right, top-to-bottom sequence, and if logical groupings are set off by lines or appropriate means, both the filling-in process and later reference to the information contained will be expedited.

The designer must be familiar with the questions being asked so that ample space will be provided for the answers. Excess space is wasteful and conveys the impression that more details should be included than are actually called for. On the other hand, too little space can make a form unusable. If, for example, a typewriter with large type will be used in filling in a list of figures, the fact must be known (some research may have to be done) so that adequate space can be assigned. And remember that handwriting, too, has to be appraised for size. Clerks' notations are usually cryptic; unless space is sufficient for a full response, the information that the form gathers may be so terse—or so compressed and difficult to read—as to be useless.

To gauge the amount of space needed on forms that are to be filled in by typewriters, it will be convenient to actually count out lines on the machine. This method will speed and simplify handling. Generally, there will be six lines to the inch if the material is single-spaced, three if it is double-spaced.

Balance is necessary for a well-designed form. The user will find it easier to read if items are nicely positioned. There is no need for information to huddle tightly in one corner of the sheet or sprawl all over.

The requirement that causes the greatest trouble is that of language. Say what you want to say as succinctly as possible; make sure that your grammar and punctuation are correct and that everyone will understand your wording. Why such attention to grammar and punctuation? Not from any schoolteacherish compulsion, but to make the language you choose convey a precise message. Incorrect grammar, punctuation, and spelling can cloud the information and defeat the purpose of the form. So can unfamiliar terminology. The simpler the presentation, the better. If a child of nine or ten can understand your sentence, it's worthy of your form; if not, try again. Sometimes it's difficult to keep language simple when space is restricted—it would be easy to fill a file with examples of "monstrosities" that point up the misuse of language in forms used by even the largest corporations. Clumsy language seems to be prevalent everywhere; yet it is both wasteful and ludicrous.

There is a single exception to the rule of simplicity in the use of language. When legal terminology is required, its cumbersome phrases and jargon—the long sentences and the unwieldy paragraphs that have evolved over the years—must be kept intact. The urge to split up long passages into more readable language must be resisted.

So here, then, are the fundamentals of form design—what may be called the "four L's" of the art: listing, layout, legibility, and language. When any one of these "L-ements" is neglected, the form will suffer.

Listing

1. Be sure to include title, subtitle, necessary dates, "to," and "from."
2. Gather all items needed for the listing; check with all users.
3. If the form will be used by a tabulating operator, be sure the data follow the fields of the tabulating cards, with appropriate field numbers.
4. Secure approval of the listing from each of the affected department heads, and from legal counsel if necessary, before going ahead to the next step.

Layout

1. Get expert help if the layout is beyond your capability—for example, to suit the optical scanner of an electronic data processing system if you have little understanding of its requirements.
2. Use cross-section or graph paper for plotting out the form. The Hammermill Paper Company makes available a form-designing kit that includes form-layout sheets marked off in boxes of two sizes: one for pica typewriter spacing, the other for elite.
3. Follow the order of the listing, taking into consideration the primary and secondary importance of items and the flow of the form.
4. Indicate the lines that are to be used to separate items, divide columns, and so on as follows:

   (a) Hairline. The thinnest line—for example, to divide a primary column into two secondary columns or mark off quantities into hundreds, thousands, and so on.
   (b) Double hairline. Two parallel thin lines, often used at the top and bottom of a tabulation or to separate a pair of primary columns.

(*c*) Half-point line. A heavier line that separates major headings, when used vertically, or divides sections horizontally for easier reading. It may be used as well to block the form, make "ballot boxes" for check marks, and so on.

(*d*) One-point line. The heaviest line practical in forms design. It is used horizontally—for example, below column heads and above a total—and vertically—as in separating captions at the left from tabulated data at the right.

5. Give the form balance to make it easier to read as well as to make it conform with the tabular stops of the typewriter that will be used in completing it.
6. Remember that the size of the form will depend on a number of factors (about which more later). But, if items are to appear on both sides of the sheet, determine whether the reverse side should be printed in book order (if bound at the left) or head to toe (if bound at the top).
7. Do not "bleed off" the page either to the left or the right with lines or text—in other words, do not extend lines or type all the way to the edge of the sheet. Also, do not position any writing above or below the portion of the page that may be required for the gripper margin if the form is to be printed by offset.
8. Determine whether the form will be placed in a binder and, if so, on which side. Leave a wide enough margin on that side to allow all the text to be read completely even when the binder is full. Indicate where holes or slots are to appear.
9. Indicate the number of copies per form and any deviation of text or layout needed to satisfy specific department requirements—including the blacking out of data which do not concern certain recipients of copies. Make a special layout for each copy that is not an exact replica of the original.
10. Choose an easily readable typeface. (This can be selected from a printer's manual or from a booklet describing cold typefaces available to a Varitypist.) Specify the type sizes for headings and other material, your preference as to "all caps" and upper and lower case, and so on.
11. Give the form a number, making sure that it doesn't duplicate any other form's number, and show the printing date and the quantity ordered if this information is desired.
12. Prepare a set of instructions for the completion and flow of the form, the length of time each department should retain its copy, and so on.

Legibility

1. Be sure the printer or Varitypist can read your layout and instructions by preparing a clean copy after all corrections have been made.
2. Leave enough room for lengthy clerical insertions to insure the form's legibility even after it is completely filled in.
3. Select the colors for the various copies of the form after first ascertaining how individual copies will be filled in. A penciled notation on dark blue paper, for example, is not easily deciphered, and ink will smudge on certain paper finishes.
4. Emphasize important elements through the use of large type, italics, underscoring, or colored ink.
5. Balance the layout, using characters that are both clear and large enough.

Language

1. Use simple, grammatical, properly punctuated, concise language unless legal requirements demand the use of special terminology.
2. Follow standard usage for abbreviations so as not to confuse the form's users.
3. Check all trade jargon before including it; that is, make sure that all terms will be understood and that they are in current use.

• • •

The design of a form depends in great measure upon the designer's knowledge of the business—or that portion of it, at any rate, with which the form deals. The designer cannot always be 100 percent right; designs may often fall flat and have to be redone, but the incidence of these mishaps can be cut down appreciably if the "four L's" are given full consideration.

There will always be special situations, such as the design of a tricky tabulating card which defies all but specialists in automatic equipment of the latest vintage. The International Business Machines Corporation or Remington Rand will furnish layout paper, but you may need the help of an engineer. It is no sign of weakness to admit that you need help in such cases; what it shows is that you are anxious to do a good job. [Numerous examples of well-designed forms are to be found in the Appendix.]*

*Bracketed material refers to original AMA publication.

ACQUISITIONS

Acquisitions is an important area for the use of well-designed forms because of the wealth of detail involved in each order, and the variety of problems which may arise in having an order filled. A good book order form can insure that an order follows a prescribed path from the initiation of the request to the purchase, and can save the library staff from unnecessary repetition of steps in the order process.

There are a variety of ways in which a library may acquire publications, including purchase, special accounts or blanket orders, and free mailing lists. This necessitates that a number of different forms be designed, or that provisions be made on a single form to accommodate these variations. The librarian needs to look ahead and try to envision most of the order situations which will arise and have a form or forms designed which will handle them easily.

Following up on orders that are not filled on a timely basis is another time-consuming aspect of acquisitions which can benefit from previously prepared letters. Again, the variety of problems which might arise needs to be taken into account. An order may need to be cancelled, or an inquiry made about a delayed order, or an incorrect invoice may need to be sent back for revision. These are just a few of the many details that form letters can handle. Depending on the volume of materials ordered, the librarian may want to have separate letters for each problem, or may combine a number of them in a checklist.

Acquisitions also has budget-related responsibilities, involving not only the budget of the library but also those of other departments for which the library orders materials. Careful record must be kept of accounts charged, totals spent, budgetary limits and so on, both for management of the current budget and for planning and projecting the next one. Additional material relating to this topic is given in the chapter on budgets.

2. Acquisitions

A. Book and Periodical Order Forms
1. Patron Requests and Recommendations
2. Orders to Vendors
3. Requests for Free Copies of Publications
4. Order Records

B. Cancellation of Orders, Follow-up on Delayed Orders, Invoice Problems

C. Miscellaneous Forms
1. Check Requests
2. Response to Purchase Recommendation
3. Searching/Ordering

D. Statistics

E. Gifts

Book and Periodical Order Forms
Patron Requests and Recommendations

PATRON REQUEST FOR BOOK ORDER
(Please Print)

AUTHOR________________________________

TITLE________________________________
EDITION________________YEAR________________

PUBLISHER________________________________

REQUESTED BY:________________________EXT.__________
COURSE RESERVE: YES__________NO__________

(SEE OTHER SIDE)

Side 1

PATRON REQUEST FOR JOURNAL TITLE
(Please Print)

TITLE________________________________
PUBLISHER________________________COST__________

REQUESTED BY:________________________EXT.__________
Would you like the Library to contact you concerning action taken? yes__________no__________
ADDITIONAL COMMENTS:
____
____

(see other side)

Side 2

Side 1

Library Material Request

REQUESTOR'S NAME		PHONE NO.	☐
COURSE/ELECTIVE		REQ'D. NLT	☐ ☐
AUTHOR(S)			
TITLE			
PUBLISHER & ADDRESS	DATE		
	EDITION		
	NO. COPIES	UNIT COST	
☐ CLOTHBOUND ☐ PAPERBOUND	ISBN		
NOTES:			
APPR. AUTH. SIGN.		DATE	

(COMPLETE FORM WITH ALL KNOWN INFORMATION)

Side 2

LIBRARY STAFF USE ONLY

☐ GENERAL COLLECTION
☐ REFERENCE
☐ REFERENCE
☐ OTHER (SEE NOTES)

LC NO. ____________
OCLC NO. ____________
CALL NO. ____________

SEARCHED
☐ CARD CATALOG
☐ ON ORDER FILE
☐ RECEIVED FILE
☐ OCLC

VERIFIED
☐ BIP
☐ PBIP
☐ BRIT BIP
☐ PUBL CATALOG
☐ PTLA

☐ DO NOT CATALOG (SEE NOTES)

☐ SPECIAL DISTRIBUTION (SEE NOTES)

SOURCE	SELECTED BY	APPROVED BY

NOTES:

ORDER DATE ____________
P.O. NO. ____________
DATE RECD ____________
VOUCHER NO. ____________

SUBSCRIPTION REQUEST

Send two copies to Library and Information Center

Title ____

____

Publisher ______________________________ Place ______________

Price __________ ISSN __________ Duration: 1 year ☐ 2 years ☐ 3 years ☐

New ☐ Renewal ☐ (Attach renewal notice and/or mailing label)

Additional Information ______________________________

Requested by ______________________ Room ________ Ext. ________

Approved by ______________________________ Date ______________

Charge to budget code no. ______________________________

Library Use Only

Order No. ____________ Date Ordered ____________ By ____________

First Issue Received ____________________ Expiration Date ____________

Address Change Required ____________________ Source ____________

BOOK OR PUBLICATION REQUEST

Send two copies to Library and Information Center

Author ____

Title ______________________________________ Edition __________

Publisher ______________________________ Place ______________

Series ________ Volume/Number ____________ No. of Copies ____________

Price ____________ LC Card No. ____________ ISBN ____________

Additional Information (Attach promotional brochure) ______________

Requested by ______________________ Room ____________ Ext. ______

Approved by ______________________________ Date ______________

Charge to budget code no. ______________________________

Library Use Only Source ______________________________

Order No. ____________ Date Ordered ____________ By ____________

PURCHASE RECOMMENDATION REQUEST

DATE __________

(PLEASE PRINT CLEARLY)

YOUR NAME ____

TELEPHONE NUMBER ______________________ ROOM NUMBER __________

To which department are you assigned? ______________________
(Medical students, please indicate MS I, II, III, IV)

Do you have a valid user's card? YES or NO (please circle one)

Please circle one of the following:

Faculty Staff
Graduate Student Medical Student

PLEASE PROVIDE AS MUCH INFORMATION AS POSSIBLE. USE A SEPARATE FORM FOR EACH TITLE REQUESTED. ALL SUGGESTIONS WILL BE CONSIDERED, HOWEVER, NO PROMISE TO PURCHASE IS IMPLIED.

Book / Journal Title: ____

____

Author / Editor: ____

Publisher: ____

Publication Date: ______________________ ISBN or ISSN: __________

PLEASE NOTIFY ME WHEN THE ITEM IS RECEIVED __________

Intended use of material (Circle one):

Patient Care

Preparation of a Review Article or Book

Dissertation Research

Definition of a Research Project or Proposal

Teaching Purposes

Other (specify): ______________________

PUBLICATION REQUEST FORM

Date of request ____________

Date needed ________________

To: Library

From: ______________________________

______________ ext: ______

Publication:

Author: ______________________________

Title: ______________________________

____

Publisher: ______________________________

Price (if purchase) __________ Date of publication ______________

U.S. Government Printing Office number (if applicable) ______________

Number of copies needed __________

Action Requested:

☐ Borrow on Interlibrary Loan for temporary use.

☐ Request free copy.

☐ Purchase:

☐ For Library (and lend to requestor for temporary use)

☐ To be retained by the requesting office

☐ For Other

Budget Coding:

☐ To be coded to Library funds.

☐ To be coded to ______________________________
(If multiple copies, please indicate correct code for each copy)

____

____

Issue Area__________

LIBRARY

Periodical Subscription Request

Please complete as fully as possible and attach any relevant brochures or literature.

Date__________

Title__________

Publisher__________

Address__________

Frequency__________ Cost P/A__________ Format__________

Number of Subscriptions__________

New, Renewal or Additional__________

Source of Information__________

Requester__________

Division__________ Telephone__________

FOR LIBRARY USE ONLY:

Division Subn.__________ Faxon No.__________

Library Subn.__________ Ulrichs__________

Circ__________ ISSN No.__________

Ref.__________ Retention__________

Notes__________

Submitted Through__________ Approved__________ Ordered__________

Issue Area__________

LIBRARY

Suggestion/Request for Purchase of Publication

Please complete as fully as possible and attach any relevant brochures or literature.

Date__________

Title__________

Author__________ Edition/Year__________

Publisher__________

Address__________ No. of Copies__________

Price__________

Source of Information/Other Identifiers__________

Comments/ Job Code__________

You will be notified when this publication is received. Please complete this section so we can contact you. Please type or write legibly.

Name__________ Division__________ Telephone__________

Current Address__________

All publications become the property of the Library and may be borrowed for 30 days. They may be renewed if no one else has requested them.

FOR LIBRARY USE ONLY

Library Staff: Please indicate sources checked.

Catalog	FB	Order Priority	Circ
On Order	ULS	FAXON	Ref
Received	Ulrichs	OCLC	
BIP	CBI	NUC	
	LC Card #	ISBN	

Submitted through__________ Approved__________ Ordered__________

RECOMMENDATION/REQUEST FOR PUBLICATION

TO ➔ LIBRARY – ACQUISITIONS

LIBRARY USE ONLY		
Control number		
Order code	Ordered by *(Name)*	
DATE		
Request received	Order placed	Order due

1. PUBLICATION INFORMATION

a. Item requested – *Mark (X) one*
- ☐ Book *(Complete items 1b–f)*
- ☐ Periodical *(Complete items 1b, c, and e–g)*

b. Title

c. Year	d. Edition	e. No. of copies
f. Price →	Unit $	Total $

g. Type of order
- ☐ Single issue

Volume	Number	Month	Year

- ☐ New subscription ☐ Renewal

Mark (X) one
- ☐ 1 year ☐ 2 years
- ☐ Other – *Describe* ____

2. AUTHOR OR ISSUING AGENCY

Name

3. PUBLISHER

a. Name

b. Telephone number

Area code	Number	Extension

Address *(Include number and street)*

c. Federal Supply Schedule No.

City	State	ZIP code

d. International Standard Book No.

4. SOURCE OF INFORMATION

☐ Mark if advertising literature attached

5. JUSTIFICATION

(Be specific)

6. USAGE OF REQUESTED ITEM *(Mark (X) one)*

a. ☐ Addition to library

b. ☐ Desk/retention copy *(Item 7 must be completed to authorize purchase)*

7. APPROPRIATION CHARGES

a. Requisitioner No.

b. Accounting codes

Division	Project(s)	Resource category	Appropriation code

SEND TO

Name		
Division or office		
Room number	Building	Telephone number

APPROVED BY
Administrative liaison or authorized person

Signature		
Title		
Division	Room number	Building
Telephone number	Date approved	

Copy distribution: WHITE – Library YELLOW – Library (Return to requester) PINK – Requester

Book and Journal Request

Library Use Only
Acquisitions

Use Separate Form for Each Item Requested

Requester ______ Emp. # ______ Tele. # ______ Mail Stop ______

Date ______ Project # ______ Dept. ______ Date Needed ______

Book

Author(s) ______

Title ______

Publisher ______ Year ______ Price ______ Call # ______

Journal Article

Journal title, vol., issue date ______

Author(s), title of article, and pages ______

Subscription

Journal Title ______

Publisher ______ Price ______

To expedite the processing of this request you may attach a copy of any matter you have regarding the item requested.

Procurement Methods

(Check appropriate boxes and obtain required approval.)

☐ Photocopy/Loan from Library Collection. If item is from Library Publication List give item # ______ and list # ______

☐ Suggest purchase for library collection. Library approval required. (If purchased, item will be available for two week loan.)

Options Below Require Approval Signature and Project #

Approval ______ Proj. # ______

☐ If necessary, obtain from another library. Cost up to $ ______ may be charged to project.

☐ Order book or journal subscription on project funds. Library will catalog item and forward it on indefinite loan.

Library Use Only
Reference

White and Yellow — Deliver to Library

Pink — To Be Retained by Requester

2

Report Request

Library Use Only
Acquisitions

Use Separate Form for Each Item Requested

Requester ______________ Emp. #________ Tele. #________ Mail Stop ________

Date ______________ Project #______________ Dept. ______________ Date Needed ________

Report No. ______________ (AD, PB, other) Report Date ______________

Author(s) ______________

Title ______________

Corp. Author (company writing report) ______________

Classification

☐ Unclassified ☐ Confidential ☐ Secret

To expedite the processing of this request you may attach a copy of any matter you have regarding the item requested.

Format Requested

☐ Paper* ☐ Microfiche

* Paper copy is always charged to the project.

Procurement Methods

Report May Be Obtained From ______________

______________ (Source)

Priority requests will be charged to project funds.
Sign this form and supply project number to be charged.

Approved ______________
Department Head, Associate, Group or Project Leader

Project # ______________

Library Use Only
Reference

White and Yellow - Deliver to Library Pink - To be Retained by Requester

TO: ACQUISITIONS DIVISION

REQUEST FOR LIBRARY MATERIALS

FROM:

PRIORITY:
ACQUISITIONS
CATALOGING

THROUGH:

AUTHOR (110) :

TITLE (310) :

EDITION (410) :
PLACE (427) :
PUBLISHER (433) :
DATE (444) :
VOL. NO. (463) :
SERIES (466) :
☐ ENTIRE SERIES WANTED ☐ ONLY THIS TITLE
PRICE (521) :
ADDITIONAL
INFORMATION :

LIBRARY LOCATION: DEPT.________________________ DATED______________

ADDITIONAL
COPY NEEDED :

WANTED ONLY IF NEW TO THIS BRANCH ☐

WANTED ONLY IF NEW TO THE SYSTEM ☐

BROCHURES
ATTACHED : ☐ YES ☐ NO

CATALOG AS A SEPARATE ☐

CATALOG AS A SERIAL ☐

PURCHASE IF EXCHANGE NOT GRANTED ☐

REPORT (TO BE FURNISHED BY ACQUISITIONS DIVISION)

☐ LIBRARY HAS COPY - CALL NO.________________
☐ TITLE IS NOT IN PRINT
☐ ORDERED
☐ EXCHANGE REQUESTED
☐ EXCHANGE NOT GRANTED
☐ ☐ SHALL WE PURCHASE?
YES NO

FOR LIBRARY USE ONLY

ACRONYM :

ORDER NO. (033) :

MIN. NO. :

SPEC. INFO. (483) :

ACCOUNT NO. (521) :

PRIORITY (60401) :

INSTR. TO CAT. (60402) :

OCLC (606) :

ASSGMENT (611) :

L.C. CARD NO. (711) :

CALL NO. (731) :

SEARCHED:

OCLC
IN PROCESS
PUB. CAT. Series
IPF
ORDERS OUT
BIP
FORTH. BOOKS
PUBL. CAT.
BROCHURE
NUC
OTHER

SERIAL REC.
ULS
ULRICHS
OTHER

ORIGINAL (WHITE COPY) - TO BE RETAINED BY ACQUISITIONS
COPY 1 (PINK COPY) - TO BE RETURNED TO ORIGINATOR
COPY 2 (BUFF COPY) -- TO BE RETAINED BY BOOK SELECTOR

LIBRARY ORDER FORM
FOR
BOOKS & PERIODICALS

DATE: __________

FROM: ______________________________ EXT: ________

QUANTITY	BOOK/PERIODICAL TITLE	START/DUE DATE

Charge Code: ____________________ Subscription Term: _____ yr(s)

Ship to Name: ______________________________

✓ Please attach the renewal notice for the periodical and/or the book advertisement. First time periodical orders take 6 to 8 weeks, depending on the publisher, to receive your first issue. I will call you when your book order arrives.

Any questions? Call me between 7:30 am and 3:45 pm

FORM.TXT

Library Subscription Order

NO. ______________________

DATE ______________________

AN EQUAL OPPORTUNITY EMPLOYER

VENDOR	SHIP TO

TITLE:

SUBSCRIPTION PERIOD: NEW:

COST: RENEWAL:

ACCOUNT CHARGED:

CHECK ENCLOSED:

COMMENTS: Please include purchase order number on all invoices and shipments.

____
LIBRARY MANAGER

****

Vendor:

COMMUNICATIONS CHANNELS, INC.
C/O PAT FRY 6255 BARFIELD ROAD
ATLANTA GA 30328

Purchase Order Number:

010290

Please show this number on all correspondence.

__Payment Enclosed $______________	__Account Number	Order Date
__Address Label Enclosed		2 JAN 90

Quantity	Description	List Price
1	TRUST & ESTATES DIRECTORY 1990	42.50

PREPAYMENT ENCLD: $42.50..PLEASE PLACE THE DIRECTORY ON STANDING ORDER...

Please direct material, invoice and correspondence to the following address, quoting the PURCHASE ORDER NUMBER:

APPROVED BY:______________________________ DATE:_____________ ACCN:

BEFORE USING THIS FORM, READ IMPORTANT INFORMATION ON REVERSE SIDE
PLEASE PRINT OR TYPE ALL INFORMATION

Customer's Telephone No.'s

Area Code | Home | Area Code | Office

ORDER FORM

MAIL TO:

Superintendent of Documents
U.S. Government Printing Office
Washington, DC 20402-9325

MasterCard VISA

Date..................

Customer Order Number......................................

Credit Card No.

FOR OFFICE USE ONLY		
QUANTITY		CHARGES
______	Publications	______
______	Subscriptions	______
	Special shipping charges	______
	International handling....	______
	Special charges.........	______
	ORPN..................	______
______	UPNS	
______	Balance Due	
______	Discount	
______	Refund	

Customer's Name and Address

ZIP

Expiration Date Month/Year

Deposit Account Number

TO PLACE YOUR ORDER BY PHONE, CALL OUR ORDER DESK AT 202-783-3238, MONDAY THROUGH FRIDAY, 8 AM - 4 PM, EASTERN TIME.

Stock No.	Quantity	Unit of Issue	List ID	Title of Publication / Subscription	Unit Price	Total

Total Enclosed: $

Ship To: (If different than above)

ZIP

Unit of Issue	Explanation
EA	Each - single copy
KT	Kit of multiple items in a special container
PD	Pad containing multiple sheets
PK	Package containing multiple copies
SE	Set of multiple items
SU	Subscription

SEE REVERSE SIDE FOR ORDERING INSTRUCTIONS

GPO Form 3430
(R 7-88) P.57532-1

INFORMATION CONCERNING YOUR ORDER OR INQUIRY

Thank you for your interest in U.S. Government publications. If you made a written inquiry, it is returned for your reference. There is no free distribution by this Office, since we are established by law as the sales agency for Government publications. We have indicated the prices of publications currently available, or have provided the information requested to the best of our ability. Unless otherwise noted, prices are for single copies, and all prices are subject to change without notice.

Payment is required in advance of shipment of publications. You may order using check or money order drawn on a bank located in Canada, the United States Possessions, in U.S. dollars. Make checks/money orders payable to the Superintendent of Documents. Checks returned by the bank as uncollectible are subject to a penalty of up to 10 percent of the amount of the check, with a minimum charge of five dollars ($5.00). You may also order, by using your VISA, MasterCard or Superintendent of Documents Prepaid Deposit Account. Do not send currency (bills or coins) or postage stamps.

Shipping is by non-priority mail. United Parcel Service, First Class and airmail services are available for an additional charge if requested. Please contact us in advance for rates if you desire this service (202-783-3238) and indicate on your order if you desire special postage.

DISCOUNTS:

With the exception of certain publications and subscriptions, a discount of 25% from the domestic price is allowed on orders of 100 or more units of issue mailed to a single address. A discount of 25% from the domestic price is also applicable on orders from bookdealers; for orders of any quantity, mailed to the dealer's business address. (The maximum discount allowable is 25%.)

INTERNATIONAL CUSTOMERS:

Mailing regulations require special handling for orders mailed to addresses outside the United States or its possessions for which we charge and additional 25% of the domestic price. Payment is required in advance by one of the methods stated above. You may also remit by UNESCO coupons or by International Postal Money Order, made payable to the Superintendent of Documents. Foreign currency and foreign checks will not be accepted. Internnational customers are allowed the same documents stated above. All orders must be in English.

Orders are sent via surface mail unless otherwise requested. Should you desire airmail service, please contact us in advance by letter, telephone (202-783-3238), or Telex (#710-822-9413, ANSWERBACK USGPO WSH.) for the total cost of your order.

TO ORDER, USE FORM ON REVERSE SIDE

1. *A separate order form must be used for ordering the following: subscription services and publications (which includes single issues of a subscription.)*
2. Type or print your complete name and address, home and office telephone numbers, date, order number (if any), Deposit Account Number (if applicable), VISA or MasterCard number and expiration date (if applicable), in proper place at the top of the form. If order is to be shipped to another location, enter address at bottom of form.
3. When ordering publications, type or print the stock number, unit of issue (see front), quantity, title, price, and total payment enclosed. ALLOW A MINIMUM OF FOUR WEEKS FOR DELIVERY (for International Orders allow a minimum of eight weeks). Mail original of form to Superintendent of Documents, Government Printing Office, Washington, DC 20402-9325.
4. When ordering a subscription, type or print the quantity, title, price, list ID (when available), and total payment enclosed. Allow 2-6 weeks, plus mailing time, for processing. All subscriptions are one year, unless otherwise noted. Subscribers will be notified by mail in ample time to renew. Mail original form to Superintendent of Documents, Government Printing Office, Washington, DC 20402-9371.
5. When ordering a specific single issue of a subscription, type or print the complete titles of the subscription, the list ID or the stock number of the issue ordered (when available), single copy price, and all data pertaining to the requested issue (issue date, volume number, issue number, etc.). ALLOW A MINIMUM OF FOUR WEEKS FOR DELIVERY (for International orders allow a minimum of eight weeks.) Mail original of form to Superintendent of Documents, Government Printing Office, Washington, DC 20402-9325.
6. Customer orders containing a credit card number or a deposit account number may be FAXED to the Superintendent of Documents on (1) 202-275-0019.
7. If the shipment is incorrect, return the shipping documentation for adjustment. DO NOT RETURN BOOK UNTIL NOTIFIED TO DO SO. ALL CLAIMS MUST BE SUBMITTED WITHIN SIX MONTHS.
8. Retain the green copy for your records.

THE FOLLOWING INFORMATION EXPLAINS HOW YOUR REQUEST WAS PROCESSED

C... We are unable to identify the publication from the information furnished.

I... This publication is not currently available. Please inquire concerning availability and price in 60 days. Inquires and orders are accepted by mail, telephone (202-783-3238), or Telex (#710-822-9413; ANSWERBACK USGPO WSH.) Our telephone order desk is staffed from 8 AM to 4 PM, Monday through Friday (Eastern Time) and will accept your VISA, MasterCard or Superintendent of Documents Deposit Account order.

L... The publication(s), subscription service(s), or single issue(s) of a subscription service you requested is out of print and no longer available from this Office.

S... The publication that you requested has been superseded or replaced by another with similar but more recent information. We have noted the new ordering information on your request.

LIBRARY REQUEST FOR UNCLASSIFIED PUBLICATIONS

To: Please address correspondence to:

Attn: Library Acquisitions

Date______________
Request No.__________

____
Authorized signature

One of the staff members of the Corporation has asked me to acquire a copy of the following publication(s):

______ Enclosed is a check in the amount of ___________ to pay for the item(s).

______ Please send complete information on price and availability.

______ Please ship and bill.

______ Ship only if item is free of charge.

For postal shipment use correspondence address at the top of the form.
For UPS shipment only use:

LIBRARY REQUEST FOR SUBSCRIPTIONS

To: Please address correspondence and shipment to:

Attn: Library Acquisitions

Date______________

____
Authorized signature

Please enter one subscription to the following journal:

______ Check enclosed in the amount of ___________.

______ Period of performance________________________.

______ Supply back issues missed.

______ Send subscription directly to the following address:

Attn:

Requests for Free Copies of Publications

Dear Publisher:

Recently we have seen a citation for your publication:

We would like to assess the scope and coverage of this
publication for inclusion in the
collection. Would you please send us a sample copy for review?

Please return a copy of this letter with the piece or indicate
on the piece that it is a sample.

Thank you for your attention to our request.

Sincerely yours,

Head, Serial Records Section
Technical Services Division

Messieurs:

Récemment nous avons lu une citation du titre:

dans la BIBLIOGRAPHIE DE LA FRANCE.

Veuillez nous envoyer un échantillon de cette publication.

Nous voulons l'examiner pour son inclusion possible dans la

collection de la

Veuillez vous agréer nos sentiments très distingués.

Head, Serial Records Section
Technical Services Division

Signor Editore:

Desideriamo esaminare la Vostra pubblicazione a scopo di inclusione

nella collezione della

Volete, per favore,

inviarci un numero della Vostra rivista a titolo di campione:

Accludete, per favore, una copia di questa lettera insieme al numero-

campione o indicate il fascicolo inviato come "campione".

Con saluti distinti,

Head, Serial Records Section
Technical Services Division

To Whom It May Concern:

We would appreciate receiving ____ copy/copies of the following:

May we be placed on your permanent mailing list to receive this publication regularly as it is issued?

Thank you very much.

RESEARCH LIBRARY

We would like to have, for the use of our research staff, the material noted below. Your kindness in sending it to us will be appreciated.

Research Library

We have not received the material listed below. As it is needed to complete our files, we would appreciate your kindness in sending it to us.

Library

We wish to acknowledge receipt of the material noted below. Thank you for sending it to the Library.

Chief Librarian.

Dear Sir:

We would greatly appreciate your adding our library to the mailing list to receive the following, without cost:

Our mailing address is:

Please notify us if there is any difficulty concerning this request or if you must charge for copies. If that is the case we shall have to resubmit the request through our purchasing office.

Thank you.

Sincerely,

Librarian

The Library has recently seen a reference to the publication cited below.

Would it be possible for you to provide this material on an exchange or complimentary basis? If so, please send it, together with any related correspondence, to the following address:

If you are unable to comply with this request, could you please supply information concerning the availability of this publication? Your assistance would be sincerely appreciated.

Very truly yours,

Exchange and Gift Unit

Greetings:

Our records indicate we regularly receive the title listed below as a gift or an exchange item, but we are missing some issues. Would you please send them or advise us if you cannot.

Title:

Problem:

( ) No issues received since:
Pas de numeros recus depuis:
Keine Numern erhalten seit:

( ) We are missing issues:
Nous n'avons pas recu les numeros:
Wir haben nichts erhalten dieses Hefte:

( ) Title has ceased. The last issue published is:

Please ship all issues to:

Thank you for your reply.

Sincerely yours,

Head, Serial Records Section
Technical Services Division

Date____________________________

TO:____

____

____

____

Our current serial records indicate that we are missing issues of the publication that has been received on an exchange basis (i.e., free of charge) from your organization entitled:

____

____

We are missing:____

____

____

Please supply all available and future issues, so that we can maintain a complete file in our library. This is not a purchase order. Do not send invoices or set up subscriptions, but supply information below:

________We will supply the missing issue(s) and all future issues.
________Missing issues are out-of-print and therefore unavailable; but we will supply all future issues as published.
________Missing issues will not be available because__________________________

____
________This title ceased publication on ______________with____________________
DATE VOLUME

Please return this completed form and publications to:

Attention__________________

Thank you for your attention to this matter. Your cooperation is appreciated.

Date:

Gentlemen:

This Library lacks the publications listed below. We will appreciate your sending this material to us at your earliest convenience.

We lack
Nos faltan
Il nous manque
Es fehlt uns

Our mailing address is:

PLEASE RETURN ONE COPY OF THIS CLAIM
WITH YOUR PUBLICATION.

Order Records

Order Record Files

Two models for PC-based systems

```
DATE OF ORDER:                  DATE RECEIVED:
TITLE:

AUTHOR:
NUMBER OF COPIES:
PUBLISHER:
ADDRESS:

TYPE OF MATERIAL:
REQUESTED BY:
P.O. NUMBER:              OR LIBRARY APPROVAL BY:
COST:                     ACCOUNT:
NOTES:
```

```
                          Record: 2762
Title                     DEBTOR-CREDITOR LAW MANUAL - 1989 SUPPLEMENT #2
Quantity                  1

Recipient/Room
Position
Recip. Address
Recip. City & St

Vendor Name               Warren, Gorham & Lamont, Inc.
Status                    On Order
Order Date                09/12/89
Total                     $ 0.00
```

PURCHASE ORDER NO. ______________ ACCN. NO. ______________

VENDOR ID. ______________ PHONE NO. ______________

TITLE ______________

AUTHOR ______________

PUBLISHER ______________

EDITION ______________ YEAR ______________

PRICE ______________ PUB. NO. ______________

REQUESTOR ______________

NO. OF COPIES ______________

ORDER REQUEST FORM

BOOK SERIAL ANNUAL (circle one)

AUTHOR/EDITOR/CORPORATE BODY: ______________

TITLE: ______________

IMPRINT: ______________
(city) (state) (publisher)

LIBRARY HAS: ______________ ISSN/ISBN#: ______________

COUNTRY: ______________ FREQUENCY: ______________ # OF COPIES: ______________

LOCATION (BRANCH): ______________ E PRICE: ______________ (per copy) FUND: ______________ VENDOR CODE: ______________

PERIOD OF SUBSCRIPTION/EDITION: ______________

RETENTION PERIOD: ______________

ROUTE TO: ______________

CALL #, COPY #, CATALOGUING INFORMATION: ______________

PUBLISHER NAME/ADDRESS (if no vendor code exists): ______________

ORDER RECORD #: .O ______________

DATE	PURCHASE ORDER NO.	REQ. NO.	GSA CONT. NO.	F.O.B.	DELY DATE
				DEST ☐ OTHER ☐	

DEPT.

APPROVAL

DATE REQUESTED	DEPT. NO.	ORIGINATOR	ACTIVITY	CODE	PHONE	PRI.	DATE MAT'L REQ'D
						06 ☐ 13 ☐	

S.O.

NSN OR MFG P/N ______ QTY. ______ U/I ______ UNIT PRICE ______ TOTAL COST ______

ITEM DESCRIPTION

J.O:

C.C:

SHIP TO:

SUGGESTED SOURCE:

ATTN: RM NO.

REP: PHONE

ADDITIONAL INFORMATION:

RECEIVED BY:

NEW TITLE__________ DATE: ____________________

TITLE ____

____

AUTHOR ____

SUBJECT ____

LOCATION ____

ESSENTIAL ____

****

PUBLISHER ____

AVAILABILITY ____

____

____

ISBN NO. ____

PRICE ____

PHYSICAL ____

CHECK NO. ____

EDITION ____

SERIES ____

REMARKS:

ROUTING LIST:

Cancellation of Orders
Follow-up on Delayed Orders
Invoice Problems

Side 1

CLAIM

Industry Association Library
Acquisition Services
Washington, D.C. 20000
202-555-7777

Order number: Date:

Order date:

Title:

Series:

Imprint: Quantity:

Message: Please ship or report, above item(s) overdue.

Use other side for response

TO:

Side 2

RETURN THIS SLIP TO SENDER AS REPORT

☐ ORDER CANCELLED ☐ ORDER ON FILE ☐ CLAIMED ITEM(S) SENT ON: ______ ☐ OTHER

Give any additional information below

☐ Out of stock	☐ To be reprinted	☐ Please confirm order	☐ Serial/set
☐ Out of print	☐ Searching	☐ Part of series	☐ Complete
☐ Not yet published	☐ Not our publication	☐ Reprint	☐ Discontinued
☐ Sold	☐ Never published	☐ Author's name incorrect	☐ Suspended
☐ New edition pending	☐ Publication date unknown	☐ Title incorrect	☐ Merged/Succeeded by *(give title below)*
☐ Probably available by ______	☐ Claimed from publisher on ______		☐ Other *(give details below)*

(Complete / Discontinued / Suspended: show last issue/date below)

ADDITIONAL INFORMATION

LIBRARY CLAIM FOR PUBLICATIONS

To: Please address correspondence to:

Attn: Library Acquisitions

Date ________

Claim No.__________ ____________________________ Authorized signature

The following was ordered from you on________________:

To date we have not received this material.

____ Please ship ordered material as soon as possible.

____ Please forward refund as material is no longer required.

____ Enclosed is proof of payment.

____ Please notify us if the item is not available at this time.

Reply requested:

LIBRARY ACCOUNT RECONCILIATION FORM

To. Please address correspondence to:

Attn:____________________

Date__________

Account No.__________________

In response to your inquiry regarding payment of Invoice #______________:

____ Please send a duplicate invoice so that we may better identify and locate the order.

____ Payment is in process. A check will be mailed to you shortly.

____ According to our records, payment was sent on or about ___________. Please notify us if proof of payment is required.

Reply:

Library

Dear Sir or Madam:

The   Library has not received the title listed, ordered____________________ on purchase order number________.

Enclosed is a mailing label for your convenience. Please ship material as soon as possible or send status report.

Thank you for your help in this matter.

Sincerely,

Acquisitions Assistant

Dear Sir or Madam:

It has been brought to my attention that ______________________________

____

which was recently received by The   Library is imperfect; pages ____ are missing.

We would much appreciate receiving a replacement copy. Enclosed is a mailing label for your convenience.

Thank you for your cooperation.

Sincerely,

Date: ____________

TO:

With reference to your/our _____shipment____invoice____letter ___statement___order (see attached)

RE:

____Payment has been held up for the following reason:

____May we return for credit/refund?
____Library discount was not applied.
____We are exempt from paying sales tax.
____Order could not be identified.
____We are unable to interpret your charges.

____You supplied:
____the wrong item.
____the wrong edition.
____incomplete set.
____insufficient number of copies.
____duplicate copies.
____defective copy.

____Lacking:

____pocket part/s
____supplement/s
____index.
____errata slip.

____Neither book(s) nor invoice received. Please advise.
____Item has already been supplied earlier and paid for.
____Item was sent unsolicited.
____Your shipment contained item/s destined elsewhere.
____Returned.
____Send itemized invoice.
____Send new invoice.
____Invoice put in line for payment.
____Deducted from invoice.
____We leave the matter open until we hear from you.

Thank you,

Acquisitions Department

In regard to ____ for:

This library _____has not received the material.

_____is holding your invoice ______________ dated

_________________ pending receipt of material.

_____hereby cancels the order.

_____has processed for payment on _______________ your

invoice________________ dated_________________

in the amount_________________.

Unless otherwise indicated, please reply/send to:

Sincerely,

Miscellaneous Forms
1. Check Requests
2. Response letter to purchase recommendation
3. Searching/ordering

Check Request
(For Accounting Dept. Use)

PAYABLE TO: ______________________________

ADDRESS ______________________________

____

____

____

____

Enclosed please find our check for $ __________ for a copy of each of the following:

SPECIAL INSTRUCTIONS TO THE ACCOUNTING DEPARTMENT

☐ ATTACHMENT TO BE MAILED WITH CHECK ☐ RETURN CHECK TO REQUESTOR ☐ MAIL CHECK DIRECTLY TO PAYEE

☐ OTHER: ______________________________

____

Account No. __________ Authorized by: ______________________________

Vendor No.:		Voucher No.:
Terms:		Purchase Order No.:
Invoice No.:		Payment Date:
Invoice Checked:	Distributed:	Keypunched:
Date:	Date:	Date:
Initials:	Initials:	Initials:

DISTRIBUTION						
Dept.	Account	Ticket No. or Work Order	Debit		Credit	

REQUEST FOR CHECK

(USE ONLY WHEN THERE IS NO INVOICE OR FOR TRAVEL ADVANCE)

Date:

Payee: *

Attention: *

Address: *

*

City — State — Zip Code

*IMPORTANT: *Check information must not exceed four lines @ 30 spaces per line.*

AMOUNT IN WORDS: ______________________ $ ________

FOR:

**Social Sec. No./Fed. Tax ID No.: [ ]

(FOR TRAVEL ADVANCE REQUEST)

ACCOUNT IDENTIFIER			AMOUNT	AUTHORIZED APPROVAL
ACCOUNT NUMBER	CENTER IDENTIFIER	SUB LEDGER		
1 9 0 3	0 0 0 0 0 0 0	X X X X X X X X		

CHARGE TO:

(FOR OTHER CHECK REQUEST)

ACCOUNT IDENTIFIER			AMOUNT	AUTHORIZED APPROVAL
ACCOUNT NUMBER	CENTER IDENTIFIER	**SUB LEDGER		
		TOTAL		

**If Required

Requested By: ______________________ Ext.: ________

Check One Box:

☐ Mail Check

☐ Send W/Attachment
(Please submit 2 copies for processing)

☐ DO NOT MAIL

Give To (Requires Approval): ______________________
Department Director Approval ______________________

FOR ACCOUNTING USE ONLY

Vendor Number ______________________ Vendor Short Name ______________________

Approved By ______________________

ACCOUNTS PAYABLE VOUCHER
(THIS VOUCHER SHOULD BE ATTACHED TO ALL INVOICES SUBMITTED FOR PAYMENT)

DATE:

PAYABLE TO: ____________________

ACCOUNT IDENTIFIER			AMOUNT	AUTHORIZED APPROVAL
ACCOUNT NUMBER	CENTER IDENTIFIER	*SUB LEDGER		
		TOTAL		

*If Required

REQUESTED BY: ____________________ EXT: __________

CHECK ONE BOX:

☐ MAIL CHECK

☐ SEND W/ATTACHMENT (Please submit 2 copies of invoice for processing)

☐ DO NOT MAIL

GIVE TO (REQUIRES APPROVAL): ____________________
DEPARTMENT DIRECTOR APPROVAL ____________________

FOR ACCOUNTING USE ONLY

VENDOR NUMBER ____________________ VENDOR SHORT NAME ____________________

INVOICE NUMBER ____________________ INVOICE DATE ____________________

APPROVED BY ____________________

TO: DATE:

FROM: Supervisor, Acquisition and Collection Development

SUBJECT: Purchase of ______________________________

Thank you for your recent suggestion for purchase for the library's collection. Upon consideration, the following action has been/will be taken:

[] Book/report will be purchased and loaned to you for 2 weeks.

[] Book will be purchased and placed in the library's reference collection. Since this collection does not circulate, you may use the book in the library. Please check with the library in 4-6 weeks regarding the status of the order.

[] Subscription will be ordered and you may check with the library in 6 - 8 weeks as to the status of the subscription. We do not have a policy of automatically routing journal issues, but you may check out issues from the library.

[] Due to limited interest/usage corporate-wide and/or cost involved, the library is unable to purchase the suggested item at this time. The item may be purchased on project funds by having the request form signed with a project number and returned to

[] Should funds become available at a later date, your suggestion will be reconsidered.

If you have any questions regarding the above, please contact

SELECTION / PROCESSING FORM

TO BE COMPLETED BY SELECTOR / ACQUISITIONS

SELECTED FOR: ____________________

PRIORITY: ____________________

CIRC. TO: ____________________

CAT. AS:

SEPARATE ____________________
SERIAL ____________________
ANALYTIC ____________________
KEEP THOSE OF INTEREST ____________________
REPLACEMENT ____________________

SPECIAL HANDLING INSTRUCTIONS / COMMENTS

____
____
____
____

WANTED ONLY IF NEW TO THIS BRANCH: ____________________

WANTED EVEN IF COPY (NO.) ____________________

WANTED ONLY IF NEW TO ____________________

WANTED FOR __________ IF NOT NEEDED ELSEWHERE

WANTED UNCATALOGED FOR ____________________

NOT WANTED FOR __________ OFFER TO __________

GIFT FROM: ____________________

ADDRESS: ____________________
____
____

ACKNOWLEDGE: YES ________ NO ________
IF NOT NEEDED RETURN TO: ____________________

SELECTOR INITIAL / DATE ________ / ________
ACQ. INITIAL/DATE ________ / ________
SERIAL RECORD:

HAS BEEN ENTERED ____________________
HAS BEEN SEARCHED ____________________
CALL NO. IS ____________________
TITLE IS ____________________
TO BE ANALYZED ____________________

SER. REC. INITIAL / DATE ________ / ________

TO BE COMPLETED BY PROCESSING STAFF

LOCATION: __________ OCLC# __________
PRIORITY: __________ 050 __________
090 __________
NAF __________
CIRC. TO: __________ RELATED __________

__________ ADDED VOLUME
__________ ADDED COPY / SET
__________ DIFFERENT EDITION

CALL NUMBER:

ENTRY (1):

	______ OLD	______ NEW	______
	______ NST	______ ULS	______
NUC	______	______	______
	______	______	______
	______	______	______

ENTRY (2):

	______ OLD	______ NEW	______
	______ NST	______ ULS	______
NUC	______	______	______
	______	______	______
	______	______	______

SEARCHER ________ / ________
________ / ________
________ / ________

DATE:
INITIALS:

SEARCHING/ORDERING FORM

MONOGRAPHS, SERIALS, CLASS SEP

OCLC :

CC:

RC:

CSR:

ASF:

CLASS SEP FILE:

OTHER:

CONTINUATION____SUBSCRIPTION____
ORDER NO:

SERIAL ID:

DESTINATION:

VENDOR NACN:

ISSN:

PRICE:

Acquisitions Statistics

IV. Purchase Orders

Type	Library			Other		
	Number (a)	Cost (b)	Backlog (c)	Number (d)	Cost (e)	Backlog (f)
1. New Subscriptions						
2. Renewals						
3. Total Subscriptions						
4. Books						
5. Print Orders						
6. Microforms						
7. Audio Visuals						
8. All Other						
9. Total (Sum of 4-8)						
10. Grand Total (Sum of 3 and 9)						

ACQUISITIONS STATISTICS

	THIS MONTH	YEAR TO DATE
TITLES SEARCHED		
GIFT VOLUMES RECEIVED		
GIFT VOLUMES ADDED		
NEW STANDING ORDERS (NON-SERIAL)		
NEW SERIAL SUBSCRIPTION TITLES PLACED		
TOTAL NEW SERIAL SUBSCRIPTIONS		
MICROFILM RECEIVED		
CASETTES RECEIVED		
OTHER AV MATERIALS RECEIVED		

MICROFICHE STATISTICS	THIS MONTH		YEAR TO DATE	
	# FICHE	VOLS. EQ.	# FICHE	VOLS. EQ.
U.S. SUPREME COURT LAW REPRINTS				
C.I.S. MATERIALS				
NEW YORK LAW JOURNAL				
FEDERAL REGISTER				
N.T.I.S. MATERIALS				
LEGISLATIVE HISTORIES				
CURRENT SESSION LAWS				
OTHER MICROFICHE RECEIVED				
TOTAL NUMBER OF MICROFICHE RECEIVED				

TECHNICAL SERVICES STATISTICS

ACQUISITIONS

Gifts	JULY	AUG	SEPT	OCT	NOV	DEC	JAN	FEB	MAR	APR	MAY	JUNE
Gift volumes received												
Gift volumes added												
Audio visual materials												
Motion pictures added												
Filmstrips added												
Cassette tapes added												
Reel-to-reel tapes added												
Videotapes added												
Phonograph records added												
Total A-V materials added												
Subscriptions												
New titles												
Total Subscriptions												
Microform materials												
Microfilm reels added												
Microfiche added												
New titles added												
Volumes-equivalent added												
Total microtext pieces added												
Documents (uncataloged)												
Volumes added												
Volumes withdrawn												
Net volumes added												
Titles added												
Titles withdrawn												
Net titles added												

ACQUISITIONS STATISTICS - MONTHLY TALLY OF ACQUISITIONS PROCUREMENTS

MONTH__________

LIBRARY STAFF									U. I. STAFF									TOTAL CUMULATIVE
BOOKS	VF/CD	PERIODICALS			SERIALS			TOTAL L.S.	BOOKS	VF/CD	PERIODICALS			SERIALS			TOTAL U.I.	
		Subs.		Single issue	S/O		Single ed.				Subs.		Single issue	S/O		Single ed.		
		N	R		N	R					N	R		N	R			

Subs. = subscription
ed. = edition

N = new
R = renewal

1/77

ACQUISITIONS STATISTICS - PROCUREMENTS

YEAR__________

CATEGORY / MONTH				JAN		FEB		MARCH		APRIL		MAY		JUNE		JULY		AUG		SEPT		OCT		NOV		DEC		TOTAL
				MT	CT	MT	CT	MT	CT	MT	CT	MT	CT	MT	CT	MT	CT	MT	CT	MT	CT	MT	CT	MT	CT	MT	CT	
LIBRARY STAFF	BOOKS																											
	VF/CD																											
	PERIOD-ICAL	Subscription	N																									
			R																									
		Single issues																										
	SERIAL	Standing Order	N																									
			R																									
		Single edition																										
	TOTAL LIBRARY STAFF																											
U. I. STAFF	BOOKS																											
	VF/CD																											
	PERIOD-ICAL	Subscription	N																									
			R																									
		Single issues																										
	SERIAL	Standing Order	N																									
			R																									
		Single edition																										
	TOTAL U. I. STAFF																											
TOTAL CUMULATIVE																												

MT = monthly total
CT = cumulative total

NOTE: Ceased/cancelled titles: to be reported in Annual Summary only.

1/77

WASHINGTON, D.C. 20560

The Libraries have received your gift copy of:

We are most grateful for your generosity.

Sincerely yours,

Acting Director of Libraries

Memorial Library
The State University
Washington, D.C. 20000

On behalf of the staff of the Memorial Library, I wish to thank you for your generous donation from your personal collection. These items are being used to update our holdings, and I am certain that they will be used and appreciated by the State University community.

For your records, I have attached a list of titles contained in your gift.

Once again, let me thank you for remembering our library with your gift. We are always anxious to receive any titles which you feel would be beneficial to our patrons.

If I can be of any assistance in the future, please do not hesitate to contact me.

Sincerely,

Side 1

GIFT AND DONATION FORM

(PLEASE READ THE DIRECTIONS FOR COMPLETING THIS FORM PRINTED ON THE REVERSE SIDE.)

DO YOU WISH TO RECEIVE AN ACKNOWLEDGEMENT LETTER FOR THIS GIFT?

____ YES   ____ NO

If you request an acknowledgement, it will be sent to you addressed exactly as you fill in the name and address blanks below. Please be sure to provide full information, in the format that you want on your acknowledgement letter.

A COPY OF THIS FORM MUST ACCOMPANY THE GIFT

NAME: ______________________________

ADDRESS: ______________________________

____

____

TYPE OF MATERIAL YOU WISH TO DONATE: ____________________

____

____

____

DATE DELIVERED : ____________________

Side 2

GIFT AND DONATION FORM

Complete this form if you have printed materials to donate The Audiovisual Form must be filled out instead for audiovisuals.

The welcomes gifts of books, journals, etc., which can be of use to our patrons. We reserve the right, however, to refuse gifts of duplicate copies of journals already in our holdings, old editions of textbooks, unless they are of historical significance, and other types of materials which do not fit into the scope of the collection.

THE CAN NO LONGER INVENTORY GIFTS, BUT will validate inventories provided by donors and return the validated list, along with a letter of acknowledgement.

IRS regulations prohibit the from making monetary evaluations of donations. However, the donor can assign his own cash value to gifts for tax deduction purposes.

Once a donation has been received, the reserves the right to DISPOSE of any items which are found to be duplicates of materials already in the collection, or which are later judged to be out of the scope of the collection. Please send any questions regarding this policy, or about possible contributions to the following address:

OR call the Acquisitions Section at the following number:

CHECK-IN LIST FOR GIFT MATERIAL

TO:	DATE

SOURCE
GIFT FROM
REMARKS

PROCESSING	
	SEARCHED. HAVE __________ COPIES.
	NOT SEARCHED.
	NEED TOTAL OF __________ COPIES.

RECOMMENDATIONS	
	RETAIN AS NEW MATERIAL.
	RETAIN AS ADDED COPIES.
	DISCARD.
	SEND TO

FROM *(Unit)*
AUTHORIZED BY

GIFT AND EXCHANGE DATA SHEET

CARD CODE ⊔⊔⊔⊔⊔ (2–6)

DATE ⊔⊔⊔⊔⊔ (70–74)

MIN ⊔ (75)

⊔⊔⊔⊔ (76–79)

P - GIFT (MONOGRAPH)
Q - EXCHANGE (MONOGRAPH)
S - G OR E (SERIAL)

AUTHOR
11001 ____________________

TITLE
31001 ____________________

DISTRIBUTION INSTRUCTIONS: ORIGINAL (WHITE) - RETAINED BY ACQUISITIONS
COPY 1 (YELLOW) - RETAINED BY SEARCH UNIT
COPY 2 (PINK) - TEMP. UNION CATALOG
COPY 3 (BLUE) - TEMP. BRANCH CATALOG

Field	Code	Columns
EDITION	41001	33–69
PLACE	42701	33–69
PUBLISHER	43301	33–69
DATE	44401	33–69
VOLUME NO.	46301	33–69
SERIES	46601	33–69
ORGANIZATION	52101	33–40
NOTES	60401	33–69
*OCLC	60601	33–40
ASSIGNMENT	61101	33–69
*L.C. CARD NO.	71101	ALPHA PREFIX 47–49; NO.PREFIX 50–51; – 52; NO.SUFFIX 53–59
CALL NUMBER	73101	33–69

OCLC USE:

CATALOG	80101	DATE (MM-DD-YY) 7–14	CALL NO. 33–52
AVAILABLE	80201	DATE (MM-DD-YY) 7–14	BINDING UNIT 33–44

CATALOGING

There are three kinds of forms used in the cataloging area: cataloging and processing worksheets, worksheets for working with a computerized, shared cataloging network, and cataloging statistics records.

Cataloging worksheets, whether for original or shared cataloging, can be useful in recording all of the vital data on a particular publication as it passes from searching to cataloging to processing. For even the most experienced cataloger, the worksheet improves consistency by providing a set format to insure that all of the necessary bibliographic and subject information is registered. Provision can be made on the worksheets for local cataloging variations. Special handling for certain categories of materials is facilitated by having boxes or lines to check on a worksheet. Libraries using OCLC or other shared cataloging systems will find a worksheet with fields and delimiters marked helpful in entering cataloging data into the system correctly. Also, processing instructions can be relayed from the cataloger without ambiguity by means of the worksheet.

Cataloging statistics forms, like other library statistics forms, are used to record a variety of data about the work accomplished.

3. Cataloging

A. Cataloging Worksheets

B. Automated Cataloging Worksheets

C. Cataloging Statistics

D. Miscellaneous Forms

1. Reclassification
2. Archives
3. On-line Change Requests

LR No. ____________________

Name ____________________

LIBRARY CATALOGING WORK SHEET

A ______ NEW BOOK
- ☐ CHECK CATALOG for "on order", previous copies, previous editions
- ☐ MAKE CARDS
- ☐ MODIFY LC CARDS

B ____ ADDED COPY

C ____ ADDED VOLUME

D ____ SUPPLEMENT

E ____ NEW EDITION

F ______ RECATALOG
- ☐ PULL CATALOG CARDS?
  ____ Yes No ____
- ☐ MAKE NEW CARDS
- ☐ MAKE SHELF LIST
- ☐ ADD CUTTER NO.
- ☐ MODIFY LC

G ______ MAKE OPEN ENTRY
- ☐ ADD TO VERSO, MAIN ENTRY
- ☐ ADD TO VERSO, SHELF LIST
- ☐ ADD TO "LIBRARY HAS" CARD, SHELF LIST
- ☐ ADD TO "LIBRARY HAS", PUBLIC CATALOG
- ☐ ADD TO RECTO, SHELF LIST

H ______ MAKE CARD NOTES
- ☐ SEE VERSO . . . MAIN ENTRY
- ☐ SEE SHELF LIST . . .
- ☐ ALSO REFERENCE
- ☐ ALSO CIRCULATION

		ALL CARDS	SHELF LIST	CARD & POCKET	SPINE
DEWEY NO.					
CUTTER NO.					
VOLUME NO.					
COPY NO.					
PART OR SUPPL. NO.					
EDITION NO.					
YEAR OF PUBL.					
CONFERENCE NO.					
YEAR OF CONFERENCE					
PLACE OF CONFERENCE					
SEASON OR DATE OF CONF.					

SPECIAL INSTRUCTIONS: ____________________

____

PRE-CIRCULATION CHECKLIST
- ______ Edition notation complete?
- ______ Full number on spine?
- ______ Identification stamp?
- ______ Catalog information on verso?
- ______ Main entry, card and pocket agree letter for letter?

Author:

Title:

Place, Publisher and Date:

# of pages:

Subject Headings:

1)
2)
3)
4)
5)
6)

Added Entries:

1)
2)

LC# or Acc. #:

CALL #: ______________________________

AUTHOR: ______________________________

TITLE: ______________________________

____

IMPRINT: ______________________________

COLLATION:

format: ____________________________

signatures: ________________________

____

____

PHYSICAL DESCRIPTION:

binding:

woodcuts, illustrations:

title pages, vignettes:

missing pages, photocopies:

other:

CONTENTS:

BIBLIOGRAPHIC REFERENCES:

SIGNIFICANCE:

PROVENANCE:

Save file # _______

OCLC # ___________

Copy number(s)

1 2 3 4

SEARCH

OCLC ___________

Local ___________

AUTHORITY

OCLC ___________

Local ___________

Recataloged? ______

LABEL(S)

Cards ordered ________

Cards received _______

Cards reordered ______

Cards received _______

PROCESSING

Labels _____________

S/L updated _________

SERIALS PROCESSING

SC350 _____________

Other records affected

____

____

____

BOOK PROCESSING "CHECKLIST"

____ DATE STAMP INSIDE COVER

____ OUR STAMP INSIDE COVER

____ AUTHOR LABEL ON UPPER LEFT CORNER OF COVER

author is ______________________________

____ LOCATION LABEL ON SPINE

location is ______________________________

____ CARD AND POCKET INSTALLED ON INSIDE BACK COVER, SHOWING
A) AUTHOR B)TITLE C)LOCATION

____ CATALOG TO TITLE

____ CATALOG TO AUTHOR

____ SHELVE

SEARCH SLIP

BOOKS & SERIALS

IN PROCESS FILE (PC AREA)____________________

ON ORDER FILE____________________

COMPLETED ORDER FILE____________________

LS/2000____________________

OCLC____________________(DATE   )

SERIAL RECORDS____________________

CONTINUATIONS____________________

AACR1____________________

SHELF LIST____________________

CATALOGING BACKLOG____________________

PREORDER:

DATE____________________SEARCHER__________

AFTER RECEIPT:

DATE____________________SEARCHER__________

COST____________________

TO: RESEARCH SERVICES
FROM: BIBLIOGRAPHIC SYSTEMS

REQUEST FOR INFORMATION

PLEASE RESPOND SWIFTLY

DATE

TO:

FROM:

CALL NO.:

AUTHOR:

TITLE:

PLEASE:

- ☐ Verify Holdings
- ☐ Return book
- ☐ Check or indicate call no.
- ☐ Revise or Re-label Should read :
- ☐ Check collation
- ☐ Indicate size __________cm.
- ☐ Note date on volume__________
- ☐ Note any edition statement__________
- ☐ Other __________

SHOULD THIS BOOK BE:

- ☐ Catalogued as: Serial Separate
- ☐ Analyzed
- ☐ Withdrawn
- ☐ Catalogued for Special Collections Which branch
- ☐ Given special handling
- ☐ Microfilmed
- ☐ Other __________

THANK YOU

TO: BIBLIOGRAPHIC SYSTEMS

FROM: RESEARCH SERVICES

REQUEST FOR INFORMATION

PLEASE RESPOND SWIFTLY

TO:

FROM:

CALL NO.:

AUTHOR:

TITLE:

CHECK ALL THAT APPLY

PROBLEM NOTED ON:

- Com Catalogue ☐
- Weekly Supplement ☐
- Card Files ☐
- Serial Record ☐
- Volume in Hand ☐

NATURE OF PROBLEM:

- Classification ☐
- Choice of Entry ☐
- Form of Entry ☐
- Descriptive Information ☐
- Missing Information ☐
- Catalogued for Wrong Location ☐
- Should Not Have Been Catalogued ☐
- Other __________

EXPLANATION OF PROBLEM:

BIBLIOGRAPHIC SYSTEMS RESPONSE:

Has been corrected

Has not been changed because:

Name __________ Date __________

BOOK ID NO.	TITLE		
00	LC NO.	AUTHOR AND CO-AUTHOR *(Editor)*	PUBLISHER
01	SYMPOSIUM, ETC, ENTRY *(If necessary)*		
	SUBJECT HEADINGS		
11	1.	2.	3.
12	4.	5.	6.
13	7.	8.	9.
20	LIB CODE	EDITION, VOLUME *(If necessary)*	PUBLICATION DATE
30	CO-AUTHOR *(Co-editor)*		

UPDATE LIBRARY BOOK HOLDINGS

(See instructions on the reverse)

52A - SIDE 1

INSTRUCTIONS

The form may be used to record either new acquisitions or to register a duplicate of another library's holdings. Note that the numbers indicated on the form correspond to the computer fields of the book holdings system.

NEW ACQUISITIONS

	BK ID NO.	Leave this space blank.
	TITLE	Enter complete title, excluding first words of "the", "a" or "an" (118 characters available).
00	LC NO.	Enter call number.
	AUTHOR etc.	Enter personal authors by surname, followed by first name and one initial. Enter co-author or co-editor simply by surname and initials. MUST ALSO COMPLETE LINE 30. For editors, include "ED" or "EDS".
	PUBLISHER	There are 20 characters available for publisher's name.
01	SYMPOSIUM	Identify symposium, sponsorship by group other than author or publisher, or other pertinent identifying information.
11	SUBJECT	List subject headings to be included.
12	"	
13	"	
20	LIB CODE	Insert numerical code for your library.
	EDITION	Specify edition, revision, volume or parts numbers (Ex: ED 2, V 1, 2).
	PUBL DATE	Enter year of publication or, if not available, year of copywrite (without "C").
30	CO-AUTHOR	List full name of co-author or co-editor: surname, forename, initials. Include "ED" if applicable.

DUPLICATES OF TITLES ALREADY IN THE SYSTEM

	BK ID NO.	This is the number appearing in the last column on the right in the computer run. Insert on the form.
	TITLE	Insert "Duplicate".
20	LIB CODE	Complete all three items on this line.

No other information is required.

52B - SIDE 2

CHECKLIST OF INFORMATION NEEDED FOR CATALOGUING FROM THE TITLE PAGE

Did you send:

xerox of title page ☐

xerox of verso of title page ☐

xerox of preface ☐

xerox of table of contents ☐

xerox of summaries ☐

xerox of cover title if different from title page ☐

Please supply the following information unless it appears on the above:

If item is lacking indicate with o

Author:____________________
Title:____________________
Place of Publication:____________________
Publisher:____________________
Date of Publication:____________________
Series:____________________
Preliminary Pages:____________________
Number of Pages:____________________
Number of Leaves:____________________
Volume Number:____________________
Number of Volumes:____________________

Type of Illustrations: Black & White: ☐

Color ☐

Maps ☐

No Illus. ☐

Other:____________________
Size:____________________
Edition:____________________
Bibliography (include inclusive pages):____________________
Index (include inclusive pages):____________________
Languages other than English:____________________

CATALOGING INSTRUCTIONS

☐ Call No.:

☐ Pull shelf card and add:

Accession No.: ________
Copy No.: ________
Notes: ____________
____
____

☐ Add supplementary notes to all catalog cards: ________
____
____

☐ Make book card and pocket

☐ Other: ____________
____
____

Send to: ________________ Cat. Div.

____ Transfer from: ______________
to: ______________

____ Catalog as separate.
____ Catalog as serial.
____ Analyze.
____ Keep those of interest.

SERIES ___ NAC needed.
____ SR card needed.
____ Has been entered in Ser. Rec.
____ Has been searched in Ser. Rec.
____ No ser. added entry to be made.
____ Ser. added entry needed.
(form below)
____ Old cat. ______ New cat.

TRACINGS

SUBJECT
Nos. __________ are in new cat.
Nos. __________ need SHAF cards.

ADDED ENTRIES
Nos. __________ are in new cat.
Nos. __________ need SHAF cards.

SOURCE
____ Gift ____ Solicited
____ Exchange ____ Unsolicited
____ Purchase

OTHER INFORMATION

LOCATION
CAT. PRIORITY

____ Circ. to:
____ Added vol. ____ Replacement
____ Added copy/set: ____ same loc.
____________ another location
____ Different ed. for ______________

CALL NUMBER

ENTRY

____ Old ____ New ____ Subject ____ NAC
____ NST ____________ LC/NUC __________
____ ULS __________
____ Serial Record __________
____ Other ______________ __________

ALTERNATE ENTRY

____ Old ____ New ____ Subject ____ NAC
____ NST ____________ LC/NUC __________
____ ULS __________
____ Serial Record __________
____ Other ____________ __________
____ Cross ref. from alternate
in LC/NUC ______________
in old cat. ________
in new cat. ________

LC CARD NUMBER

Acq. initials __________ ; date __________ Searcher's initials __________ ; date ________

SELECTION SLIP CAT. PRIORITY ____________

1a. Wanted for ____________ only if new to this branch.

1b. Wanted for ____________ only if new to this branch.

2a. Wanted for ____________ even if copy two (or more? ______).

2b. Wanted for ____________ even if copy two (or more? ______).

3a. Wanted for ____________ only if new to system.

3b. Wanted for ____________ only if new to system.

4a. Wanted for ____________ uncataloged.

4b. Wanted for ____________ uncataloged.

5. Wanted for ____________ if not needed elsewhere.

6a. Not wanted for ____________ . (Please use this space if it is possible that a conflict of interest could occur.)

6b. Not wanted for ____________ .

6c. Not wanted for ____________ .

7. Offer to ____________ .

8. Assign to ____________ . (for Exchange Section use only)

9. Gift: if dup or not wanted, return to ____________

Comments:

PLEASE INITIAL AND DATE

Instruction slip for typist
from cataloger

PLEASE TYPE:

___ STENCIL
___ Set of cards for catalog
___ Shelf list
___ Call numbers, subject headings and added entries for catalog set and shelf list

___ Blue preliminary catalog card and slips
___ Acquisition slip
___ White preliminary shelf list
___ L.C. order & pink carbon
___ L.C. order number on order & pink carbon

___ Complete book cards
___ Book cards (orange/yellow)
___ Book cards (reference - blue lined & yellow)
___ Book cards (blue - unlined and yellow)
___ Book card (White lined - RFF)

___ Continuation: holdings, acquisition slip and book cards
___ Added copy: holdings and book cards

___ Add House or Senate reports, etc.to Hearings

___*Purchase for__________
___ Send to______________

Search in:

___ NUC ___ CBI ___WR
___ Monthly Catalog

Other:

FINAL ROUTING	CATALOGING PRIORITY
	SEARCHER
	DATE OF SEARCH

CRITERIA

1. Author	☐ NOT ESTABLISHED ☐ ESTABLISHED (NO CONFLICT) ESTABLISHED AS: ____________	
	REFERENCE FROM NAME ON PIECE ☐ NO REFERENCE MADE SEE: ____________ SEE ALSO: ____________	
2. Title	☐ NOT IN CATALOG ☐ IN CATALOG ☐ ON HOLDING SHELF ☐ PRIORITY	NUMBER OF COPIES
3. Edition	☐ ANOTHER EDITION IN LIBRARY CALL NUMBER: ____________ SUBJECTS: ____________ ____________ ____________ ☐ ON HOLDING SHELF ☐ PRIORITY	
4. Series	☐ CARDS MADE FORM OF ENTRY: ____________	
5. Library of Congress card	☐ NO LIBRARY OF CONGRESS CARD LIBRARY OF CONGRESS CARD NUMBER: ____________	

TREATMENT DECISION

1. Duplicates	☐ KEEP INDEFINITELY ☐ KEEP TEMPORARILY → ☐ DISCARD	NUMBER OF COPIES
2. New editions	☐ KEEP ALL ☐ KEEP LATEST KEEP: ____________	
3. Catalog as:	☐ MONOGRAPH ☐ SERIAL ☐ COLLECTED SET	
4. Library of Congress card	☐ ORDER ☐ DO NOT ORDER	
5. Accession list card	☐ PREPARE ☐ DO NOT PREPARE	

GIFT PUBLICATION DECISION

TEMPORARY SHELFLIST CARD

CALL NO.______________________________

AUTHOR:______________________________

TITLE:______________________________

BORROWER:______________________________

DATE BORROWED:______________________________

Classification:

AUTHOR:

TITLE:

Send to:

Borrow for:

Purchase for:

XXX CORPORATION
LIBRARY PROCESSING FORM

DATE:
Please complete your appropriate section and forward the form onto the next person.

TO: ACQUISITIONS ASSISTANT

A. Title ______________________________
____

B. Priority ___ Complete By ________

C. **Order Type:**
Original ___
Added Copy ___
Stand. Ord. ___
Tickler's File ___
New Ed. or Annual w/o std. ord. ___
Donation by ______________________

D. **Publication Type:**
Monograph ___
Serial ___
Loose-Leaf ___

E. Catalog w/call no. _____ w/o call no. _____

F. To card & pocket:
All copies _____
Lib. copy _____
Needs name labels on spine _____

To be checked out to ______________________
Has been checked out to ______________________

G. **Location:**
Library ___
Reference ___
Mag.Display___
Other ___
Personal copy owned by ______________

H. **Medium:**
Print ___
Microform ___
Audio/Visual ___
Software ___

I. Copy Numbers _____

J. Add multi-copies note to catalog ____________

3) **Serial Holdings:**
Begins with v. ____, no. ____ Date____________
Ends with v. ____, no. ____ Date____________

4) **Frequency** ______________________

5) **How Supplemented?** ______________________
____

6) **Route? (Y/N)** _____
If Y, specify _____Original ____Copy Rpt.Ltr.
_____Copy ____Copy T/C
_____Orig.Rpt.Letter

Publication is routed to: ________ ________ ________

________ ________ ________ ________ ________

7) **Bind? (Y/N)** ____
8) Add to EBSCO Order? (Y/N) ____
9) **OCLC Searched ? (Y/N)** ______

TO: LIBRARIAN:

1) **Serial Counsel Union List Record**:
For serials to be retained more than 1 yr., make an OCLC workform & submit to CAPCON. File workforms in Counsel Workforms binder.

2) **Serial Retention** (Serials are issued annually or more frequently. Looseleafs do not need retention data, except for their news summaries)
____ Keep all issues
____ Keep current issue only
____ Other________________________________

TO: CATALOGER:

Please refer to Acquisitions Assistant and Librarians sections above for cataloging. If Sec. D is marked as "Serial," forward this form w/catalog screen print and item to Serials Asst. After the form is returned to you use the Serials Assistant section to complete the catalog record and forward this form w/catalog screen print to the Processing Assistant.

TO: SERIALS ASSISTANT:

Please make a serial record for this title to include the appropriate information. Fill in the acronym in this section and return this form w/catalog screen print to Cataloger.

Acronym ______

TO: PROCESSING ASSISTANT

1. Please use the information on the catalog screen print attached to produce card and pocket labels. 2. If Sec. C is marked as "Added Copy," refer to Catalog Screen Print for label format. 3. If Sec.J-7 is Yes, set up a record for it in the Bindery Manual. 4. If publication type is SERIAL, file this form with catalog screen print in "Processing Forms Completed " File.

Automated Cataloging Worksheets

OCLC: REC STAT:-------- ENTRD:-------- USED:--------

TYPE:______ BIB LVL:______ GOVT PUB:______ LANG:______ SOURCE:______ ILLUS:______
REPR:______ ENC LVL:______ CONF PUB:______ CTRY:______ DAT TP:______ M/F/B:______
INDX:______ MOD REC:______ FESTSCHR:______ CONT:______
DESC:______ INT LVL:______ DATES:______

NUMBER TAG	1st ind	2nd ind	DATA ELEMENT	TEXT
010			LC CARD NUMBER	
020			ISBN	
040			CATALOGING SOURCE	
041			MULTI-LING OR TRANS	
050			LC CALL NUMBER	
090			LOCAL CALL NO.	
049			HOLDINGS	
1_ _			MAIN ENTRY	
2_ _			TITLE	
250			EDITION	
260			IMPRINT	
300			COLLATION	
4_ _			SERIES	
5_ _			NOTES	
6_ _			SUBJECTS	
7_ _			ADDED ENTRIES	
8_ _			SERIES TRACED DIFFERENTLY	

SERIALS WORKSHEET

Govtpub:_____ *Lang:_____ Source:_____ S/Lent:_____ Repr:_____ *Enclvl:_____ Confpub:_____

*Ctry:_____ Sertp:_____ Alphabt:_____ Indx:_____ Modrec:_____ Physmed:_____ Cont:_____

*Frequn:_____ Pubst:_____ *Desc:_____ Cumind:_____ Titlpag:_____ ISDS:_____ Regulr:_____

Dates:__________-9999

---

1 010*****______________________________

3 022*****______________________________

6 092*****_______________$b_______________

7 049*****______________________________

8 1__ __*__ __**______________________________

____

9 2__ __*__ __**______________________________

10 245*__ __**______________________________

____

____

11 250*****______________________________

12 260*__ __**______________________________

____

13 300*****______________________________

14 362*__***______________________________

15 4__ __*__ __**______________________________

____

16 5__ __*__ __**______________________________

17 6__ __*__ __**______________________________

18 6__ __*__ __**______________________________

19 6__ __*__ __**______________________________

20 7__ __*__ __**______________________________

21 7__ __*__ __**______________________________

22 8__ __*__ __**______________________________

```
OCLC: NEW          Rec stat: n  Entrd: 880222         Used: 880222
Type:     Bib lvl:   Govt pub:    Lang:      Source:   Leng:
          Enc lvl:   Type mat:    Ctry:      Dat tp:   MEBE: 0
Tech:     Mod rec:        Accomp mat:
Desc:     Int lvl:   Dates:         ,
  1 010
  2 040               ǂc
  3 007              ¦b  ¦c  ¦d  ¦e  ¦f  ¦g  ¦h
```

AUDIO-VISUAL MATERIALS

NUMBER TAG	1st ind	2nd ind	DATA ELEMENT	TEXT
010			LC CARD NUMBER	
020			ISBN	
040			CATALOGING SOURCE	
041			MULTI-LING OR TRANS	
050			LC CALL NUMBER	
090			LOCAL CALL NO.	
049			HOLDINGS	
1_ _			MAIN ENTRY	
2_ _			TITLE	
250			EDITION	
260			IMPRINT	
300			COLLATION	
4_ _			SERIES	
5_ _			NOTES	
6_ _			SUBJECTS	
7_ _			ADDED ENTRIES	
8_ _			SERIES TRACED DIFFERENTLY	

NAME:__________ DATE:__________

```
OCLC: NEW            Rec stat: n Entrd: 880212        Used: 880212
Type:    Bib lvl: m Lang:       Source: _ Accomp mat:
Repr:    Enc lvl:   Ctry:       Dat tp: _ MEBE: 1
         Mod rec:   Comp:       Format: n Prts: n
Desc: _  Int lvl:   LTxt:       Dates: ____,
  1 010                                           SOUND RECORDINGS
  2 040           ¦c SMI
  3 007           ¦b  ¦c  ¦d  ¦e  ¦f  ¦g  ¦h  ¦i
```

020			ISBN	
040			CATALOGING SOURCE	
041			MULTI-LING OR TRANS	
050			LC CALL NUMBER	
090			LOCAL CALL NO.	
049			HOLDINGS	
1_ _			MAIN ENTRY	
2_ _			TITLE	
250			EDITION	
260			IMPRINT	
300			COLLATION	
4_ _			SERIES	
5_ _			NOTES	
6_ _			SUBJECTS	
7_ _			ADDED ENTRIES	
8_ _			SERIES TRACED DIFFERENTLY	

TECHNICAL REPORT CATALOGING FORM

FIELD NAME	TAG	FIELD CONTENTS
Year($c)	008	$c
MMDD($d)	008	$d
Report No.	037	$a
(Repeatable)	037.2	$a
	037.3	$a
Doc. Control #	088	$a
Conference ($n=no., $d= date, $c=place)	111	$a
Title : $b Subtitle	245	$a
Report Date	260	$a
Page Count	302	$a p.
Contents Note	505	$a
Classification	506	$a
(Repeatable)	506.2	$a
	506.3	$a
Local Note	590	$a
Descriptor (Repeatable)	653	$a
	653.2	$a
	653.3	$a
	653.4	$a
Subject Headings (Repeatable)	690	$a
	690.2	$a
	690.3	$a
Personal Author (Repeatable)	700	$a
	700.2	$a
	700.3	$a
Corporate Author	710	$a
Title Added Entry	740	$a

OCLC SEARCH SLIP

__ SERIES ______________
__ MONOGRAPH ______________
__ ANALYTIC ______________

LC CALL NO.

MAIN ENTRY (AUTHOR OR TITLE)

CD. CAT :
GS
LC
DATA BASE:

SERIES STATEMENT(4XX FIELD)

SUBJECT HEADING

PERSONAL NAME ADDED ENTRIES
(700 XX FIELD)

CD. CAT. :
GS
LC
DATA BASE:

SERIES M.E. (8XX FIELD)

Online cataloging screen
Software: Q & A (Symantec)

```
       TITLE:


      AUTHOR:
SHELF LOC:
   EDITION SERIES:                       VOLUMES:
            PLACE:                     PUBLISHER:
       NO. COPIES:                          YEAR:
           OFFICE:                         PAGES:
       DATE REC'D:
  LOCATION IN LIB:
            OTHER
```

Online cataloging screen with sample record display

```
  Title[1]
AlpNumb.Ini Year   Last1
```

```
                              LIBRARY CATALOG
CLASSIFICATION:         Alpha:   Alp
                        Number:  Numb
                        Initial: .Init
                        Year:    Year         Info:  Info
AUTHOR(S):
 L1: Last1                                                  First1
 L2: Last2              First2
 L3: Last3              First3
 L4: Last4              First4
TITLE:     Title[1]
           Title[2]
           Sub: Subtitle
PUBLISHER:      Place:  Place
                Pub:    Publisher
                Date:   Date
NOTE:      Note[1]
           Note[2]

SUBJECT:   1st  Subject1
           2nd  Subject2
           3rd  Subject3
```

```
                              LIBRARY CATALOG
  CLASSIFICATION:       Alpha:   HF
                        Number:  1042
                        Initial: .U5
                        Year:    1987       Info:
  AUTHOR(S):
   L1: Office of Management and Budget
   L2:
   L3:
   L4:
  TITLE:    Standard Industrial Classification Manual. 1987 ed.

            Sub:
  PUBLISHER:      Place:  Washington, DC
                  Pub:    U. S. Department of Commerce
                  Date:   1987
  NOTE:


  SUBJECT:  1st
            2nd
            3rd
```

NOTIS NEW AUTHORITY RECORD WORKFORM

Created by __________ date __________ Input by __________ date __________

Cleared by __________ date __________ Revised by __________ date __________

SF# FMT A R/TYP z DT XX/XX/8X R/DT none STAT nn E/LEV n
SRC d LANG ƀƀƀ ROM n MOD UNIQUE __ GOVT ƀ S/SYS n D/I n NUM n S/TYP n
NAME a SUBJ a SER b AUTH a H/ESTAB a T/EVAL a IP a RULES c

NOTE: If your heading is a personal name, enter a lowercase "a" after subfield UNIQUE. If your heading is a corporate or other non-personal name heading, enter a lowercase "n."

040::FHM ǀc FHM

Library of Congress Class Number

053:: ______________________________ ǀb ______________________________

Established Heading

1____: __ __: ______________________________

____

See-From References

4____: __ __: ______________________________

____

4____: __ __: ______________________________

____

4____: __ __: ______________________________

____

See-Also Reference

5____: __ __: ______________________________

____

Source Data Found

670:: ______________________________

Local Note: your initials and date

690:: ______________________________ tamp

Revised 11/13/87

REGIONAL CAMPUS NOTIFICATION FORM

From: SF Initials: _______ Date: ___/___/8__

To: _____

NOTIS Authority Record Control Number: _______________

Headings errors observed in the following NOTIS Bibliographic Records:

_______________ _______________ _______________ _______________ _______________

_______________ _______________ _______________ _______________ _______________

_______________ _______________ _______________ _______________ _______________

Remarks: ____

____

Cataloging Statistics

CATALOGING STATISTICS FOR THE MONTH OF __________

ACTIVITY		WK 1	WK 2	WK 3	WK 4	WK 5	TOTAL
CATALOGING							
Monographs Original:	Titles Volumes						
Modified:	Titles Volumes						
Serials Original	Titles Volumes						
Modified	Titles Volumes						
LOCAL DATA RECORDS	Created Modified Deleted						
AUTHORITY RECORDS							
Added entries:	Created Modified Deleted						
Subject headings:	Created Modified Deleted						
SHELFLIST CARDS Filed Pulled							
ITEMS PROCESSED							
ITEMS WITHDRAWN							
Records modified							
Records deleted							

TECHNICAL SERVICES STATISTICS
CATALOGING

	JULY	AUG	SEPT	OCT	NOV	DEC	JAN	FEB	MAR	APR	MAY	JUNE
1. Titles cataloged for copy												
2. Titles originally cataloged												
3. Titles recataloged												
4. Titles reclassified												
5. Volumes reprocessed												
6. Titles withdrawn												
7. New volumes added												
8. Replacement volumes added												
9. Total added volumes (7+8)												
10. Volumes mutilated												
11. Volumes withdrawn												
12. Volumes declared lost												
9 -												
11 + 12												
Growth in volumes												

Statistics for the Week of ______________________

CATALOGING

Books	Titles	Volumes
New Titles:		
Original Cat.		
Cataloging from L.C. Copy		
Added Copies		
Continuations		
Reclassifications		
Total		
Withdrawn and Lost		
Corrections		

Documents

New Titles ______________________

Lost ______________________

Processing

Books ______________________

Documents ______________________

Initials ______

QUARTERLY REPORT - CATALOG RECORDS DEPARTMENT

QUARTER ENDING: ___ ___ ___ ___ FISCAL YEAR : ____
Dec. Mar. Jun Sep.

TITLES PROCESSED:	THIS QUARTER					YEAR TO DATE				
	CATALOG/ INPUT		OTHER			CATALOG/ INPUT		OTHER		
	Orig	Mod	Tran	Adds	W/D	Orig	Mod	Tran	Adds	W/D
MONOGRAPH (Books)										
OTHER:										
SERIALS (Books)										
OTHER:										
TOTALS										
GRAND TOTALS										

RECORDING SHEET - AUTOMATED BIBLIOGRAPHIC CONTROL UNIT

I. Titles catalogued

	this quarter					
	new cataloguing			recataloguing		
	OCLC x-cat	copy input	added v or c	OCLC x-cat	copy input	added v or c
MONO-GRAPHS Hardcopy						
Micro-form						
SERIALS Hardcopy						
Micro-form						
OTHER (specify)						
TOTALS						

II. Titles catalogued for affiliates

III. Searching

	FOUND IN OCLC			MAN. SEARCH PERFORMED
	LC record	member record	not verified	
Cataloguing searching				
Pre-order searching				

rev. 4/2/81

QUARTERLY REPORT - ORIGINAL INDEXING UNIT

rev. 9/25/81

Quarter ending: ___ ___ ___ ___ Fiscal Year _____
dec mar jan sep

I. Titles catalogued

	this quarter				year-to-date			
	new cataloguing		recataloguing		new cataloguing		recataloguing	
	orig	mod	orig	mod	orig	mod	orig	mod
Monographs Rare*								
Microform								
Others								
Serials Rare*								
Microform								
Others								
Other (specify)								
TOTALS	a	b	c	d	e	f	g	h
GRAND TOTALS	a+b+c+d =				e+f+g+h =			
Serial adjustments, serial record, major problems								

* Include x-catalogued rare in "mod" columns.

II. Totals compared with expected

	this quarter	year-to-date
1. GRAND TOTALS (from I)		
2. EXPECTED NUMBER		
3. Line 1 - line 2		

	this quarter	year-to-date
III. Titles catalogued for affiliates		

I. Volumes in Book Stacks, Periodicals, and Other Collections
(Count by Volume)

Type		1st of Month(a)	Added(b)	With-drawn(c)	End of Month(d)	Back-log(e)
1. Monographs (Excluding Microforms)	3.01					
2. Serials (Excluding Microforms)	3.01					
3. Periodicals (Bound)	3.02					
4. Periodicals (Unbound)	3.04					
5. Periodicals in Microform	3.05					
6. Maps						
7. All Other						
8. Total						

II. Titles Held in All Collections (Count by Title)

		1st of Month(a)	Added(b)	With-drawn(c)	End of Month(d)	Back-log(e)
1. Monographs (Printed)	4.01					
2. Monographs (Microforms)	4.01					
3. Serials (Printed)	4.01					
4. Serials (Microform)	4.01					
5. Periodicals (Printed)	4.03					
6. Periodicals (Microform)	4.03					
7. Maps						
8. All Other	4.07					
9. Total (Printed) (Sum of 1,3,5)						
10. Total (Microform) (Sum of 2,4,6)						
11. Grand Total (Sum of 9 & 10)	4.08					

III. Cataloging (Work Not Shown in Tables I and II)

Operation	Added (a)	Backlog (b)
1. Analytics		
2. Recataloging (Monographs)		
3. Recataloging (Serials)		
4. Recataloging (Periodicals)		
5. Mats		
6. Card Sets		
7. Card Filing		
8. Revision		

Cataloging: Miscellaneous Forms

1. Reclassification
2. Archives
3. On-line change requests

Original Call #		Revised	
Class #	Book #	Class #	Book #

PROCESS IN: ____________

ARCHIVES

ACCESSION RECORD

PROVENANCE: ____________________ ACCESSION NO.: ____________

DESCRIPTION: ____________________

____

____

____

DATE RANGE: ____________________

QUANTITY: ____________ LOCATION/DISPOSITION: ____________

____________ ____________

ACCESS CONDITIONS/COPYRIGHT: ____________________

____

____

REMARKS (ARRANGEMENT, CONDITION, ETC.) ____________________

____

____

____

CONFIDENTIAL DETAILS: ____________________

DONOR/PREVIOUS CUSTODIAN: ____________________

ADDRESS: ____________________

PHONE: (H) ____________ (W) ____________

CONTACT: ____________ PHONE: ____________

COMPILED BY: ____________ DATE: ____________

TYPE CODE CHANGE REQUEST

INSTRUCTIONS

1. Complete form and return it to OCLC Online Data Quality Control Section or to your Network Office.
2. Print in ink or type clearly.
3. In **Submitted by**, give name of person to whom questions should be referred. Be sure the name is legible.
4. When submitting a list that has accumulated over a period of time, re-check to verify that requested changes are still necessary.
5. See *Cataloging: User Manual* (section 12.2.2.1) for more detailed information.

REPORTED BY (OCLC SYMBOL) ________

DATE ________

PHONE (   ) ________ X ____

SUBMITTED BY

____

	OCLC CONTROL NUMBER	INPUTTING LIBRARY	FROM TYPE	TO TYPE
1.				
2.				
3.				
4.				
5.				
6.				
7.				
8.				
9.				
10.				
11.				
12.				
13.				
14.				

COPY FORM AS NEEDED

BIBLIOGRAPHIC RECORD CHANGE REQUEST

☐ TYPE CODE CHANGE ☐ FILING INDICATOR CHANGE ☐ O-LEVEL RECORD

OCLC CONTROL NO. ____________

LC CARD NO.
(010 ǂa) ____________

INSTRUCTIONS

1. Complete entire form and return it to OCLC Online Data Quality Control Section or to your Network Office.
2. Print in ink or type clearly. Underline parts to be changed.
3. See *Cataloging: User Manual* (section 12.2.2) for more detailed information.
4. Staple photocopy of proof for changes, if necessary, in upper left corner: 3×5 in. copy or smaller to front; larger items to back.
5. If no proof is attached, cite authority for change.

INPUT BY
(OCLC SYMBOL 040 ǂc) ____________

REPORTED BY
(OCLC SYMBOL) ____________

NAME ____________

DATE ____________

AUTHOR
(1xx)

TITLE
(245 ǂa)

FIXED FIELD	FIXED FIELD CODE:			
	REQUESTED CHANGE:			

LINE NO. __ __ TAG __ __ __	TEXT FROM RECORD: REQUESTED CHANGE:
LINE NO. __ __ TAG __ __ __	TEXT FROM RECORD: REQUESTED CHANGE:
LINE NO. __ __ TAG __ __ __	TEXT FROM RECORD: REQUESTED CHANGE:
LINE NO. __ __ TAG __ __ __	TEXT FROM RECORD: REQUESTED CHANGE:

FOR OCLC USE ONLY

COPY FORM AS NEEDED

DUPLICATE RECORD REPORT

INSTRUCTIONS

1. Complete form and return it to OCLC Online Data Quality Control Section or to your Network Office.
2. Print in ink or type clearly.
3. When submitting a list that has accumulated over a period of time, re-check to verify that requested changes are still necessary.
4. See *Cataloging: User Manual* (section 12.2.2.3) for more detailed information.
5. Use a different Duplicate Record Report form for each bibliographic format.

REPORTED BY (OCLC SYMBOL) ____________

DATE ____________

FORMAT: ____________

PREFERRED RECORD	DUPLICATE RECORDS			
	1	2	3	4

COPY FORM AS NEEDED

INCORRECT FILING INDICATOR REPORT

INSTRUCTIONS	
1. Complete form and return it to OCLC Online Data Quality Control Section or to your Network Office. 2. Print in ink or type clearly. 3. When submitting a list that has accumulated over a period of time, re-check to verify that requested changes are still necessary. 4. See *Cataloging: User Manual* (section 12.2.2.2) for more detailed information.	REPORTED BY (OCLC SYMBOL) ________________ DATE ________________

	OCLC CONTROL NUMBER	IF SERIAL, PLEASE INDICATE	FIELD TAG	INCORRECT INDICATOR	CHANGE TO
1.					
2.					
3.					
4.					
5.					
6.					
7.					
8.					
9.					
10.					
11.					
12.					
13.					
14.					

COPY FORM AS NEEDED

CIRCULATION

Circulation forms, which are used to check-out, transmit, and retrieve materials, are as individual as the circulation systems of the libraries themselves. While some kind of charge slip and overdue notice is used in most libraries, the details on those forms will depend largely on the lending policies of the library. Special libraries and special collections, because of their size and the nature of the service they provide, display a much wider variety of lending procedures and regulations than academic and public libraries. Some of that variety can be seen in the charge cards and transmittal forms which some libraries send in the book being borrowed. Libraries also use cards as the transmittal vehicles for explaining lending policies.

In keeping with their position within bureaucracies and business organizations, many special libraries have developed overdue notices in the form of memoranda or letters as opposed to the traditional post card-sized notice. Requests for the return of publications are usually explained by noting that other staff members need the material, rather than that an arbitrary due date has arrived.

Circulation statistics, the traditional measure of library service, are often kept in great detail by special libraries. Those libraries whose budget support comes from various offices within their organization have particularly good reason to keep careful statistics demonstrating that staff are using the services for which the office is paying. Circulation statistics, which are kept by the subject matter of the materials borrowed, serve as both an acquisitions and weeding guide for the library manager.

4. Circulation

A. Charge Cards

B. Transmittals to Accompany Books

C. Overdue Notices

D. Miscellaneous

E. Statistics

Charge Cards

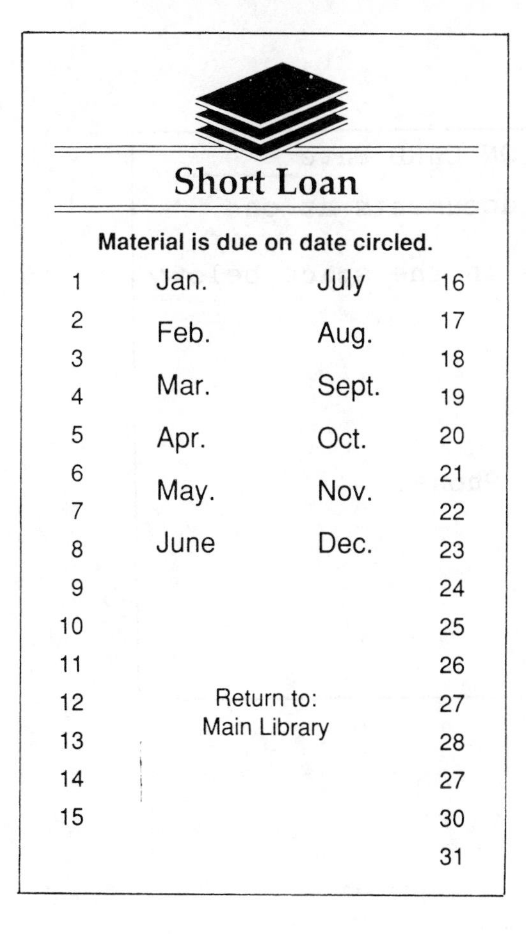

Short Loan

Material is due on date circled.

1	Jan.	July	16
2	Feb.	Aug.	17
3			18
4	Mar.	Sept.	19
5	Apr.	Oct.	20
6	May.	Nov.	21
7			22
8	June	Dec.	23
9			24
10			25
11			26
12			27
13			28
14			27
15			30
			31

Return to:
Main Library

AUDIO / VIDEO CASSETTE
CHARGE RECORD

Title ______________________

____

____

____

Borrower ______________________

Tel. ext. ______________________

Date borrowed ______________________

FASTEN PINK COPY OF FORM
TO MATERIAL; LEAVE OTHER
COPIES ON LIBRARY DESK.

Cassette loan period is two weeks.

Library

Title of Periodical	
Vol. and No.	Date of Periodical
Date Borrowed	Date Due
Borrower's Name, Mail Code, Phone No.	
NOTES:	

Central Library

Check Out Slip
In the absence of staff

Name ______________________

Employee # ______________________

Date ______________________

Book or Report:

Call # ______________________

Title ______________________

____

Journal:

Title ______________________

____

Issue date ______________________

Leave slip in circulation box

READING ROOM CIRCULATION CARD Date_____

Document request limit - 10 documents at one time.

List accession numbers in the space below

1.	6.
2.	7.
3.	8.
4.	9.
5.	10.

Requested by: Phone:

Address:

Organization:

PC Software Charge Record

Standard Loan Is Two Weeks.

Bar Code: ☐☐☐☐☐ ☐☐☐☐☐☐☐☐

Pkg. Name ____________________

No. of Diskettes: __________ **No. of Manuals:** __________

Borrower: ____________________ **Ext.:** __________

Employee No.: ____________________ **Dept.:** __________

Proj. No.: __________ **Proj. Leader:** __________

Date Returned: __-__-__

Date Borrowed: __-__-__

__________ **Days @ $1/Day=**
$

I will not make any copies and acknowledge responsibility for the return of both documentation and diskettes for the above software.

AUTHOR RESERVE

TITLE

DUE	NAME
	OFFICE TELEPHONE
	NAME
	OFFICE TELEPHONE
	NAME
	OFFICE TELEPHONE
	NAME
	OFFICE TELEPHONE

1 Mar 70

RETRIEVAL NO. ________

DOCUMENT AUTHOR ________

DOCUMENT NO. ________

DOCUMENT DATE ________

YOUR NAME ________

EXTENSION ________

DATE BORROWED ________

RECALLED ________

RESERVES 1. ________

2. ________

3. ________

DOCUMENT CHARGE CARD

AUTHOR

TITLE

DATE DUE	BORROWER'S NAME	ROOM NUMBER

NAME:

ROOM: EX:

AUTHOR	TITLE	D. DUE
	ACTION FORM A-736 (10/75)	

* QUICK CHARGE *

Leave this card on the shelf in place of the book you take.
Remove the card and cross-off your name, etc. when you re-shelve the book.

Classification number or report number	Title	Borrower's name and phone number	Date charge

Author

Title

Date of Publication

Permanently Charged to ______________________
Division or Office

Signature of Borrower ______________________

Date Borrowed ______________________

Rm. No. ________ Ext. ______

Long term loan from Central Library

Call No. ______________________ Date ______________

____
Author

____
Title

____ Division

____ Employee

LIBRARY CHARGE SHEET

PLEASE FILL IN ALL COLUMNS. IF YOU ARE CHARGING MORE THAN ONE ITEM, YOU MAY USE DITTO MARKS IN THE APPROPRIATE PLACES.

DATE DUE ______

PLEASE PRINT

CARD NO.	BORROWER'S NAME	PHONE NO.	BUREAU/ DIVISION	ROOM NO.	CALL NO.	COPY NO.	TITLE	AUTHOR	LANG-UAGE

Transmittal Forms to Accompany Book

TO:

The library has a waiting list for this material. It is requested that the material be returned by

________________ .

–RETURN PROMPTLY–

DATE DUE: ________________

THERE IS A RESERVE LIST FOR THIS PUBLICATION.

TO: ________________

____

____

Building: ________________

Room: ________________

THIS PUBLICATION **MUST** BE AVAILABLE DURING OFFICE HOURS.

Do not transfer to another person without first notifying the Library.

TO: Library

LIBRARY ROUTING CARD

RETURN TO:

HAND CARRY ONLY

DATE DUE: ______________________

TO: ______________________

____

____

Building: ______________________

Room: ______________________

THIS PUBLICATION **MUST** BE AVAILABLE DURING OFFICE HOURS.

Do not transfer to another person without first notifying the Library.

LIBRARY ROUTING CARD

HAND CARRY ONLY

Return publication by

SPECIAL MESSENGER to:

DATE DUE: ______________________

TO: ______________________

____

____

Building: ______________________

Room: ______________________

THIS PUBLICATION **MUST** BE AVAILABLE DURING OFFICE HOURS.

Do not transfer to another person without first notifying the Library.

LIBRARY ROUTING CARD

RETURN TO:

TO:

LIBRARY BOOKS MUST BE KEPT IN THE OFFICE DURING WORK HOURS

PLEASE NOTIFY THE LIBRARY IF YOU LEND THIS BOOK TO ANOTHER STAFF MEMBER. YOU ARE RESPONSIBLE FOR ANY BOOK LISTED IN YOUR NAME.

PLEASE RETURN BOOKS AS SOON AS POSSIBLE. OTHERS MAY BE WAITING TO READ THEM.

REFERENCE	3332 3333
CIRCULATION	
Books	3332
Periodicals	3322
Govt. statistical releases	3342
INTERLIBRARY LOAN	2317
GOVT. DOCUMENTS	3334

RESEARCH LIBRARY
STOP 102

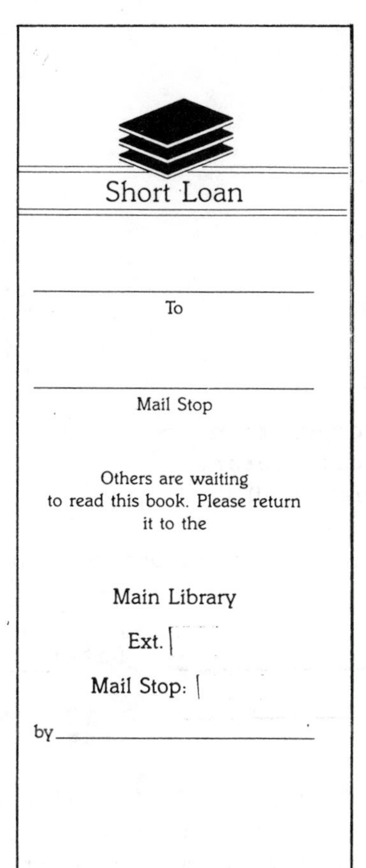

Short Loan

To

Mail Stop

Others are waiting to read this book. Please return it to the

Main Library

Ext.

Mail Stop:

by

LIBRARY

extension

DATE DUE:

The Library has more than books.
Flip over to see a list of other services.

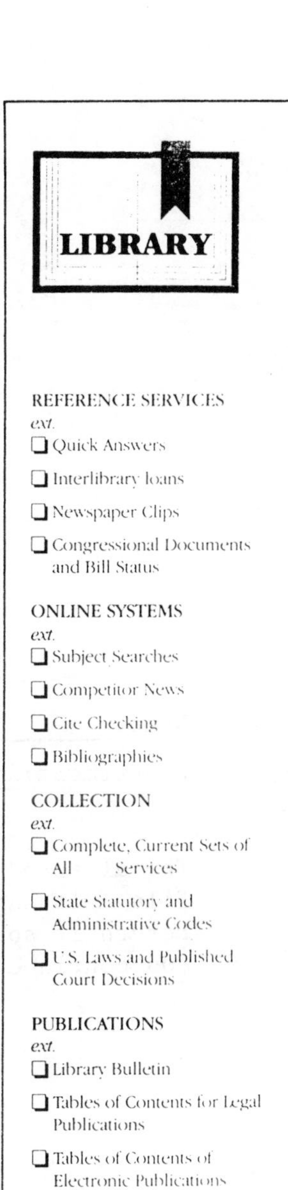

LIBRARY

REFERENCE SERVICES
ext.
- ❑ Quick Answers
- ❑ Interlibrary loans
- ❑ Newspaper Clips
- ❑ Congressional Documents and Bill Status

ONLINE SYSTEMS
ext.
- ❑ Subject Searches
- ❑ Competitor News
- ❑ Cite Checking
- ❑ Bibliographies

COLLECTION
ext.
- ❑ Complete, Current Sets of All Services
- ❑ State Statutory and Administrative Codes
- ❑ U.S. Laws and Published Court Decisions

PUBLICATIONS
ext.
- ❑ Library Bulletin
- ❑ Tables of Contents for Legal Publications
- ❑ Tables of Contents of Electronic Publications
- ❑ Library Alert

BOOK AND SUBSCRIPTION ORDERS
ext.

XXX Corporation
Technical Library
Washington, D.C.

Responsibility for material signed out of library

Name:______________________________ Date:______________

Department:______________________________

The attached material has been entered into the Technical Library circulation file. It has been signed out to your account. When you are finished, please return it so that we may clear our records. If you give it to someone else, you continue to be responsible for its return.

Thank you.

The Industry Association **MEMORANDUM**
Washington, D.C.

TO: Individuals on attached library routing DATE:
slip for______________________________

FROM: Central Library, Serials Desk

SUBJECT: Retrieval of ______________________________issues.

Another staff member has immediate need for these periodicals. Please check your desks, in-boxes, files, etc. to see if you might still have them.

Their quick return to the library will be appreciated by your colleagues!

Thank you.

Memorandum

TO :

DATE:

IN REPLY REFER TO:

FROM : Library, Room

SUBJECT: Overdue Books, Periodicals

The publications listed below are overdue and should be returned to the Library.

Material checked Not Renewable has other requests awaiting or has been borrowed from another library.

Please return or renew books on or prior to date due, as this makes them more available to all, and saves the sending of notices.

Publication	Date Borrowed	Date Due	Not Renewable	Please Renew

PREVIOUS EDITION IS OBSOLETE

Library

TO

FROM:
CIRCULATION DESK

☐

☐

OVERDUE

WE SHALL APPRECIATE YOUR RETURNING THIS MATERIAL WHICH

☐ HAVE RESERVES WAITING

☐ ARE OVERDUE—BORROWED FOR YOU FROM ANOTHER LIBRARY (WE ARE OBLIGATED TO RETURN SUCH BORROWED MATERIALS ON TIME)

☐ WILL BE ON RESERVE READING SHELVES

☐ WAS LOANED FOR OVERNIGHT USE ONLY

Overdue Recall

NOTICE OF OVERDUE BOOKS AND PERIODICALS DATE

NAME OF BORROWER

ITEMS OVERDUE: SHORT TITLE AND AUTHOR	DATE DUE

THE ITEM(S) LISTED ABOVE ARE OVERDUE AS OF THIS DATE.

PLEASE RETURN THEM TO THE LIBRARY AT YOUR EARLIEST CONVENIENCE.

I have a continuing need for this material and would like the loan extended for:

1 week 2 weeks 1 month

I no longer have the material in my possession. Explanation:

FURTHER COMMENTS

Industry Association Library
Book & Periodicals Collection
Circulation Desk, Room 100
Ext. 4444

MEMORANDUM

TO:

DATE:

The material listed below is charged to you. Is it still in use?

Due date:

Please respond by RETURNING, RENEWING, or TRANSFERRING to ______________.
Please telephone if you have questions. Thank you for your assistance.

TEXT OF CIRCULATION NOTICES

RECALL NOTICE - This notice is just to alert you that we now have a waiting list for the material listed below. Please return it no later than the due date shown below.

Thank you.

TEXT OF CIRCULATION NOTICES

FIRST NOTICE - The material listed below is now overdue. If no longer needed, please return it to the Research Library. If you wish an extension, please call x or .

Thank you.

TEXT OF CIRCULATION NOTICES

SECOND NOTICE - There has been no response to our first recall notice for the material listed below. We need your cooperation. If this material already has been returned to us, please call .

Thank you.

Industry Association Library
Book & Periodicals Collection
Circulation Desk

MEMORANDUM

TO:

DATE:

FROM: , Resource Librarian

SUBJECT: Final overdue notice

The library material listed below is long overdue. A careful search of our circulation records and bookshelves indicates that the material still has not been returned.

You will understand that the return or replacement of loaned material is essential to the continued effectiveness of the library. In order to clear your record with the library, please either return the material immediately or obtain a replacement copy (copies) for the library. For your convenience, we have included order or replacement information next to each title listed below.

All staff members leaving the Association must have a clearance form signed by the library staff before receiving their final paycheck. The form will only be signed if all material charged to you is accounted for. It is easier if this matter is settled now rather than on your last day.

Please give this matter your prompt attention. Thank you.

XXX Corporation
Central Library
Circulation Desk
Room 100, Ext. 4444

MEMORANDUM

TO:
LOCATION:

Date:

SUBJECT: Return of library material

The publication(s) noted below have been requested by another reader. We would appreciate their prompt return. If you wish you may request them again at a later date.

If you have questions or problems relating to this request, please call the circulation desk at ext. 4444. Thank you for your cooperation.

Call number	Author	Title

MISSING
FROM THE LIBRARY !

PLEASE RETURN ASAP

THANK YOU

Library	TO (PLEASE BRING THIS NOTICE WITH YOU)	FROM: CIRCULATION DESK ☐ ☐

THE PUBLICATION(S) LISTED BELOW WILL BE HELD FOR YOU UNTIL ____________

Notification of Reserve Material

MEMORANDUM

TO: DATE:

FROM: Technical Library
Circulation Desk, Room 100

SUBJECT: Requested material

The publication indicated below has been received by the library.
It will be held on reserve for you for 5 work days and then reshelved.

Call Number Author Title

NEW BOOK

DATES:

THIS BOOK WILL BE ON DISPLAY DURING THE ABOVE DATES. IF YOU WOULD LIKE TO BE NOTIFIED WHEN IT IS READY TO CIRCULATE, PLEASE LEAVE YOUR NAME, DEPARTMENT AND TELEPHONE NUMBER BELOW.

NAME	DEPT.	PHONE NO.

CALL NUMBER

LIBRARY NEW BOOK RESERVE

PLEASE LEAVE THIS FORM IN BOOK

AVAILABLE FOR LOAN

IF YOU WISH TO BORROW, SIGN BELOW

PLEASE PRINT

NAME *(First, Initial, Last)*	ROOM NUMBER	EXTENSION

DATE

TO: ______________________________

FROM: ______________________________, Reading Room

The attached is sent for your retention:

/___/ because we believe it will be of interest to you.

/___/ in answer to your request.

It has not been included in the collection. However, if you feel that it should be made a permanent part of the collection, please return it with the form below when you no longer need it. Otherwise, please DO NOT return it to the Reading Room.

DATE

TO: Reading Room ______________________.

This item should be retained in the Reading Room's collection because ____

____

____

____.

Statistics

STATISTICS

I CIRCULATION:

A. Materials loaned

	Books	Theses	Periodicals	Total
Staff				
Other libraries				
Total				

B. Materials borrowed from other libraries

Books

Periodicals

II TECHNICAL PROCESSES:

A. Books ordered for staff

B. Books cataloged

New books

Annuals

Name__________

Date__________

PUBLIC SERVICES SECTION

Circulation

	Loans From Library								Books Used In Library	Loans To Library	Photocopy (Items)			Shipping Items
	Bureau				Outside						Bureau		Outside	
	Census	Other Books	Other Period.	Total	Census	Other Books	Other Period.	Total			Tables of Contents	Other		
M														
T														
W														
T														
F														
M														
T														
W														
T														
F														
M														
T														
W														
T														
F														
M														
T														
W														
T														
F														
M														
T														
W														
T														
F														
Total														
Code	VI 1	VI 2	VI 3	VI 4	VI 5	VI 6	VI 7	VI 8	VI 11	VI 12	VI 13	VI 14	VI 15	VI 17

DOCUMENT LOAN PROGRAM FISCAL WEEK ____________

Starting Request Backlog ________________

Number of requests received ________________

Number of requests processed ________________

Number of Documents Loaned ________________

Ending Request Backlog ________________

DOCUMENT LOAN PROGRAM FISCAL WEEK ____________

Starting Request Backlog ________________

Number of requests received ________________

Number of requests processed ________________

Number of Documents Loaned ________________

Ending Request Backlog ________________

DOCUMENT LOAN PROGRAM FISCAL WEEK ____________

Starting Request Backlog ________________

Number of requests received ________________

Number of requests processed ________________

Number of Documents Loaned ________________

Ending request backlog ________________

DOCUMENT LOAN PROGRAM FISCAL WEEK ____________

Starting Request Backlog ________________

Number of requests received ________________

Number of requests processed ________________

Number of Documents Loaned ________________

Ending request backlog ________________

5

INTERLIBRARY LOAN

Since many special libraries treat interlibrary loan as an integral part of circulation, librarians should use this chapter in conjunction with the one on circulation. Interlibrary loan statistics are kept on circulation forms by most libraries. For those librarians who want to keep a separate record of Interlibrary Loan (ILL) statistics, an example is provided in this chapter.

The standard interlibrary loan form is the basis of the procedure. These are available from library supply firms. Libraries can have their name and address printed on them to save time. One such example, included in this chapter, provides for most of the communication needs of libraries seeking to borrow from one another. The advantage of such standardization, in terms of time and ease of operation, is apparent to most librarians. Consequently no interlibrary forms other than the standard one have been included.

The same uniformity is not apparent in the ways in which special libraries lend books acquired on interlibrary loan to their patrons. Although most choose one kind of a slip to be inserted in the book, a variety of rules, regulations, and warnings are printed on them. Often the forms are $8^1/_2$" or more in length, so they will be taller than the average book for greater visibility. Some are reversible, so the patron who has finished with a book can turn the slip upside down to signal routing back to the library.

Also included in this chapter are examples of forms used to receive requests for interlibrary loans and to record the search strategy used in locating a library having the title. The special obligation imposed on libraries borrowing material on interlibrary loan has led a number of them to develop special overdue notices used just for delinquent interlibrary loans.

5. Interlibrary Loan

A. Loan Requests

B. Loan Replies

C. Transmittals to Accompany Outgoing Loans

D. Transmittals to Accompany Loans Charged to Patrons

E. Overdue Notices

F. Interlibrary Loan Statistics

Borrowing Library

Fill in left half of form including both library addresses in full

Fold here

Send sheets A, B and C to lending library and enclose shipping label

Lending Library

Fill in pertinent items under REPORTS, return sheets B and C to borrowing library

ARNOLD GRAPHIC IND INC 14599

Date of request

Call No.

A

REQUEST

For use of **Status** **Dept.**

Author (or periodical title, vol. and year)

Title (with author & pages for periodical articles) (Incl. edition, place & date) ☐ **This edition only**

Verified in (or source of reference)

If non circulating, please supply ☐ Microfilm ☐ Hard copy if cost does not exceed $ ______

Note: The receiving library assumes responsibility for notification of non receipt

Standard [illegible] Interlibrary Loan Code Library of Congress [illegible]

AUTHORIZED BY: ______
(FULL NAME)
Title ______

INTERLIBRARY LOAN REQUEST

According to the A.L.A. Interlibrary Loan Code and the Federal Library Committee's I.L.L. Code

REPORTS: Checked by

SENT BY: ☐ Library rate ☐ ______

Charges $ ______ Insured for $ ______

Date sent ______

DUE ______

RESTRICTIONS: ☐ For use in library only

☐ Copying not permitted ☐ ______

NOT SENT BECAUSE: ☐ In use

☐ Non circulating ☐ Not owned

☐ ______

Estimated Cost of: Microfilm ______

Hard copy ______

BORROWING LIBRARY RECORD:

Date received ______

Date returned ______

By ☐ Library rate ☐ ______

Postage enclosed $ ______ Insured for $ ______

RENEWALS: (Request and report on sheet C)

Requested on ______

Renewed to ______
(or period of renewal)

☆ GPO 1969—O-340-464 #70J

Interlibrary Loan Request

Requestor's Name	Office Symbols	Phone Number	Date

Complete this side if you are requesting a Book.	Complete this side if you are requesting a Periodical.
Author	Title
Title	Volume Year
Publisher	Article
Date	Author
	Pages

Verification *(To be completed by the Circulation Technician)*

Sources

Call Number

Action Taken

INTERLIBRARY LOAN REQUEST

DATE: ______ NAME: ______ EXT.: ______

PROJECT: ______

DEPARTMENT: ______

PLEASE PROVIDE ALL AVAILABLE INFORMATION

BOOK – AUTHOR: ______

TITLE: ______

PUBLISHER & DATE: ______

YOUR SOURCE FOR THIS INFORMATION: ______

PERIODICAL ARTICLE

TITLE OF PERIODICAL: ______

VOLUME: ______ DATE: ______ PAGES: ______

TITLE OF ARTICLE: ______

AUTHOR OF ARTICLE: ______

YOUR SOURCE FOR THIS INFORMATION: ______

PLEASE INDICATE A DEADLINE FOR RECEIVING THIS MATERIAL: ______

I.L.L. DESK: CONTACTS/NOTES

Interlibrary Loan Request for PERIODICALS

PERIODICAL TITLE

REQUESTER
ROOM
EXT.

REQUEST DATE

REQUEST NO.

VOL. NO.	ISSUE NO.	DATE	PLACE OF PUBLICATION

ARTICLE TITLE

PAGES

ARTICLE AUTHOR(S)

PHOTOCOPY ACCEPTABLE
☐ YES ☐ NO

REQUIRED BY (DATE):

SOURCE OF REFERENCE WITH VOL. & PAGE NO.

PURPOSE OF BORROWED MATERIAL:
___ WORK ___ CLASS WORK
___ OTHER

CONSIDER FOR PURCHASE?
☐ YES ☐ NO

LIBRARY USE ONLY

ISSN:

LENDING LIBRARY

LOCATED

FILLED

DUE

RENEW REQUESTED

RENEWAL DUE DATE

RECALLED

RET'D TO LENDER

NOTICE: WARNING CONCERNING COPYRIGHT RESTRICTIONS

The copyright law of the United States (Title 17, United States Code) governs the making of photocopies or other reproductions of copyright material.

This institution reserves the right to refuse to accept a copying order if, in its judgment, fulfillment of the order would involve violation of copyright law.

Interlibrary Loan Request for BOOKS

TITLE

REQUESTER
ROOM
EXT.

REQUEST DATE

REQUEST NO.

AUTHOR(S)

DATE/EDITION

THIS EDITION ONLY?
_____ YES _____ NO

PUBLISHER

PLACE OF PUBLICATION

PURPOSE OF BORROWED MATERIAL:
___ WORK ___ CLASS WORK
___ OTHER

CONSIDER FOR PURCHASE ?
_____ YES _____ NO

REQUIRED BY (DATE):

SOURCE OF REFERENCE WITH VOL. & PAGE NO.

LIBRARY USE ONLY

IL:

LENDING LIB.	CALL NO.

LOCATED

FILLED

DUE

RENEW REQUESTED

RENEWAL DUE DATE

RECALLED

RET'D TO LENDER

NOTICE: WARNING CONCERNING COPYRIGHT RESTRICTIONS

The copyright law of the United States (Title 17, United States Code) governs the making of photocopies or other reproductions of copyright material.

INTERLIBRARY LOAN REQUEST

JOURNAL ARTICLE

Journal Title ____________________

Volume __________ Date __________ Pages __________

Author of Article ____________________

Title of Article ____________________

____

BOOK OR MONOGRAPH

Author or Editor ____________________

Book Title ____________________

Publisher __________ Date __________ Pages __________

Author of Article (if applicable) ____________________

Title of Article ____________________

WHERE DID YOU SEE THIS REFERENCE CITED? ____________________

Do you have a library user's card? YES or NO (circle one)

Your Name ____________________

Your Department ____________________ Telephone ____________________

I have read the warning on copyright restrictions
and I accept full responsibility for compliance.

____
(YOUR SIGNATURE)

NOTICE
WARNING CONCERNING COPYRIGHT RESTRICTIONS

The copyright law of the United States (Title 17, United States Code) governs the making of photocopies or other reproductions of copyrighted material.

Under certain conditions specified in the law, libraries and archives are authorized to furnish a photocopy or other reproduction. One of these specified conditions is that the photocopy or reproduction is not to be "used for any purpose other than private study, scholarship, or research." If a user makes a request for, or later uses, a photocopy or reproduction for purposes in excess of "fair use", that user may be liable for copyright infringement.

This institution reserves the right to refuse to accept a copying order if, in its judgment, fulfillment of the order would involve a violation of copyright law.

REQUEST FOR INTERLIBRARY LOAN - BOOK
(Please Print)

Date: ____________________

AUTHOR/EDITOR ____________________

BOOK TITLE ____________________

____

PUBLISHER ____________________

PUBLICATION DATE ____________

REQUESTED BY ____________________ STOP ______ EXT ______

DO NOT WRITE BELOW

OCLC SEARCH: ____, ____, ____, ____, ____, ____, ____, ____, ____

LIBRARY	DATE	STATUS
1.		
2.		
3.		
4.		

REQUEST FOR INTERLIBRARY LOAN -- JOURNAL
(Please Print)

Date: ____________________

JOURNAL ____________________

YEAR, VOLUME, PAGES ______, ______, ______

ARTICLE TITLE ____________________

ARTICLE AUTHOR ____________________

REQUESTED BY ____________________ STOP ______ EXT ______

DO NOT WRITE BELOW

OCLC SEARCH ____, ____, ____, ____, ____, ____, ____

LIBRARY	DATE	STATUS
1.		
2.		
3.		
4.		

INTERLIBRARY LOAN REQUEST

	LIBRARY STAFF ONLY
REQUESTER: ______	
PHONE: ______ BLDG/RM #: ______	
TODAY'S DATE: ______ DATE NEEDED: ______	il: ______
CHECK ONE:	OCLC #: ______
☐ BOOK REQUEST:	LOC: ______
BOOK TITLE: ______	
______	
BOOK AUTHOR: ______	REQ: ______ __ __
☐ PERIODICAL REQUEST:	REC: ______ __ __
PERIODICAL TITLE: ______	DUE: ______ __ __
ARTICLE TITLE: ______	RET'D: ______ __ __
ARTICLE AUTHOR: ______	
VOL: ______ NO: ______ DATE: ______ PP: ______	

PLEASE NOTE: ANY PATRON WITH OVERDUE INTERLIBRARY LOAN MATERIALS WILL NOT RECEIVE NEW ILL MATERIALS UNTIL OVERDUES ARE RETURNED OR RENEWED.

INTERLIBRARY LOAN
WORK SHEET

Name	Department	Phone	Date

BOOK

Author:
Title:
Date:

PERIODICAL

Name:
Date:

SOURCES CONTACTED	RESPONSE	DATE	SOURCES CONTACTED	RESPONSE	DATE

ILL PHONE REQUEST

Date________________

Name____________________________ Phone________________

Address____________________________

____

____

Material Requested

Periodical____________________________

Year__________ Volume__________ Pages__________

Author____________________________

Title____________________________

____

__________PICK-UP

__________SENT __________TOTAL PAGES

__________NOT OWNED/CANCEL __________NAME

REQUEST RECEIVED THRU OCLC	OCLC NUMBER	ILL NUMBER
CALL NUMBER		ORGANIZATION CODE
AUTHOR		
TITLE		
DUE DATE	DATE RECEIVED	DATE REQUESTED
ARTICLE		
PATRON	ROOM NUMBER	TELEPHONE NUMBER
LENDING LIBRARY		LENDING CHARGES $
RETURN TO		

Loan Replies

Central Library
Document Delivery System

WE REGRET THAT WE ARE UNABLE TO FILL YOUR INTERLIBRARY LOAN REQUEST FOR THE FOLLOWING REASON:

Material requested is: ___not owned ___not yet received ___in circulation ___non-circulating ___lost/missing ___at bindery

___ Proper payment coupon is not attached to request.
___ Citation is incomplete. Missing item(s)___________________________
___ Citation is incorrect. Please verify.
___ Request form is not checked as to copyright compliance.
___ Other___________________________

YOUR REQUEST IS BEING:

___ Returned. Please correct problems indicated above and resubmit.
___ Referred to___________________________
___ Other___________________________

Date__________Signed_________________________(202)xxx-xxxx

Author: Date:

Title:

We have received your request for the above Publication. Regretfully all copies are out on loan to other members at the present time. We shall, however, send you a copy as soon as one is returned to the library.

If we can be of any further help to you please feel free to contact us at any time.

LIBRARY

Public Information Center
Washington, D.C. 20000

Please note our response as checked below:

( ) We are please to enclose the documents you requested. Please return them via first class mail by __________ with a copy of the interlibrary loan form attached so that we may clear your records.

( ) Documents marked with a "No" on your ILL Form/letter are not available on our interlibrary loan program. ( ) Your request forms are enclosed.

( ) The documents marked with an "R" on your ILL Form/letter are currently in use and will be loaned to you as soon as available.

( ) We do not loan documents directly to individuals. Please resubmit your request through your public, university, or department library on the standard American Library Association interlibrary loan request form. Request attached. Documents marked with an "L" on your letter are available on our loan program.

( ) We are unable to supply documents noted on your ILL Form/letter with an "M" as loans. However, we have furnished you with free microfiche copies which you may keep.

( ) Please use the address noted below on all interlibrary loan forms and in all future interlibrary loan correspondence.

( ) Please sign your interlibrary loan forms. We must have a valid signature rather than initials so that we are aware of who within your library or organization is taking responsibility for the documents.

( )

Should you have questions, please contact our interlibrary loan department at the address below or by calling (202)xxx-xxxx.

Public Information Center
ATTN: Loan Department
P.O. Box 000
Washington, D.C. 20000

THE INDUSTRY INSTITUTE
5000 M Street, N.W.
Washington, D.C. 20000

Member Information Service
(202)XXX-XXXX

Member:

Date due:

Material on loan:

The Industry Institute maintains the Member Information Service as a focal point for the collection and dissemination of materials about the industry. We are pleased to be able to serve you by lending you the material listed above. Please return it as soon as you have reviewed it so that it will be available to others.

1. Please return the material to the Member Information Service by the due date shown above, with this loan slip. If an extension is needed, contact the department.

2. Return ring binders and other bulky items in rigid containers or padded envelopes (you might want to re-use the envelope in which this material was sent to you).

3. If you should develop your own printed materials, please forward copies of them to the Member Information Service. This will help us be sure the files are continually updated and remain fresh and relevant.

Date prepared:

Prepared by:

Remarks:

Transmittals to Accompany Outgoing Loans

DO NOT REMOVE FROM BOOK

TO:

DUE:

Inter-library Loan Policies of
the Library

Materials should be returned by messenger or insured parcel post.

No more than three items may be borrowed at one time.

The loan period for books is two weeks. One two-week renewal may be requested.

Periodicals are loaned for one week and are not renewable.

RETURN TO:

LIBRARY

LIBRARY LOAN

TO: ______________________

____

____

____

____

DATE DUE: ______________________

Please return the following book(s) by messenger/in a JIFFY BAG, INSURED FOR $100.00 return receipt requested.

2-PART FORM

INTERLIBRARY LOAN

Borrower: ______________________

____

Due Date: ______________________

Please Note

Loaned material is subject to recall

Messenger service should be used for pickup and delivery of material

Reverse this form when returning item borrowed

Return To:

TO:

INTERLIBRARY LOAN

This book has been borrowed from the RESEARCH LIBRARY

It should be returned by

____

It is lent with the understanding that it will be returned immediately if needed by the Staff.

RESEARCH LIBRARY

TO:

Transmittals to Accompany Loans Charged to Patrons

INTERLIBRARY LOAN

This publication is lent to the firm with the understanding that it will be returned immediately upon demand.

Do not take it from the building.
Do not leave on book truck.

RETURN BY HAND TO THE LIBRARY

11th Floor · Reference Desk

By ____________________

Interlibrary Loan

____
To

____
Mail Stop

This is a loan through the courtesy of

____________________Library.
(Do not detach form from material)

Return Due:____________________.

Library Services
Ext.
Mail Stop:

TO:

INTERLIBRARY LOAN

This book was borrowed from another library, and must be returned on:

PLEASE RETURN THIS VOLUME IN A MESSENGER ENVELOPE TO THE RESEARCH LIBRARY, STOP 102

DO NOT REMOVE FROM BOOK

INTERLIBRARY LOAN

TO:

WE HAVE BORROWED THIS ITEM
FROM ANOTHER LIBRARY AT YOUR
REQUEST AND MUST RETURN IT ON:

PLEASE RETURN IT TO THE RESEARCH
LIBRARY CIRCULATION DESK BEFORE
THAT DATE.

FAILURE TO OBSERVE THE ABOVE
DEADLINE WILL JEOPARDIZE OUR
BORROWING RELATIONS WITH OTHER
LIBRARIES AND MAY PREVENT US FROM
OBTAINING OTHER BOOKS FOR YOU.

BORROWED FROM:

RETURNED ON/BY:

ILL #

TO: ____________________

FROM: THE LIBRARY

DUE IN LIBRARY ON OR BEFORE

____

THIS MATERIAL WAS BORROWED FOR YOU ON INTERLIBRARY LOAN FROM AN OUTSIDE LIBRARY. IT SHOULD BE KEPT AVAILABLE DURING OFFICE HOURS, SINCE IT IS SUBJECT TO RECALL BY THE LENDING LIBRARY AT ANY TIME.

BORROWED FROM: ____________

____

PLEASE DO NOT REMOVE THIS SLIP

For the use of

____

Date due

____

THIS ITEM WAS BORROWED FOR YOU ON INTERLIBRARY LOAN.

The safety of borrowed material is the responsibility of the borrower. In case of loss or damage, the borrower is obligated to meet all costs of repair or replacement, in accordance with the preferences of the lending library.

To:

Return to Library
by ______________________.

This material has been borrowed on Inter-library Loan for your use. Inter-library Loan is a courtesy arrangement between libraries which is maintained by compliance with the policies of the lending library. Please help us by observing these guidelines:

- Due dates must be strictly observed
- Borrowed items must be hand-carried, never mailed
- Loose issues of periodicals are to be used in the library only
- Borrowed items are subject to recall and must be kept immediately available during working hours
- Under no circumstances should a borrowed item be taken outside the city

To: Library

To: ______________________

Mail Room: ______________________

Date Due: ______________________

Interlibrary Loan

This publication was borrowed for your use from an outside Library. Please keep it available during office hours for recall at any time.

This book is charged to you and is NOT transferable without notifying the Headquarters Library.

Please return on or before date due.

Return to:

THIS MATERIAL WAS LOANED TO THE
LIBRARY.

FROM: ____________________

PATRON: ____________________

YOU ARE RESPONSIBLE FOR RETURNING ALL MATERIALS BORROWED ON INTERLIBRARY LOAN TO THE **LIBRARY** ON TIME AND IN THE CONDITION IN WHICH RECEIVED.

DUE DATE ____________________

YOU ARE ALSO RESPONSIBLE FOR PAYING FOR ANY LOST, MISPLACED OR DAMAGED MATERIALS. FAILURE TO DO SO MAY RESULT IN DENIAL OF BORROWING PRIVILEGES TO YOU AND

PLEASE DO NOT REMOVE THIS BAND.

PLEASE RETURN TO

XXX Corporation
Technical Library

MEMORANDUM

TO:

DATE:

LOCATION:

FROM: Office of the Librarian, Technical Library
Room 100

SUBJECT: Interlibrary loan materials you ordered

We have called your office twice regarding interlibrary loan materials being held for you at the Technical Library circulation desk in Room 100.

We have a commitment with the lending library to return these materials soon. The materials will be held at the circulation desk until _____________ and then returned to the lending library.

If you have any questions regarding this notice, please contact the circulation desk on XXX-XXXX.

DESCRIPTION OF MATERIALS:

Public Information Center
Washington, D.C. 20000

Dear

This letter is to remind you that you have overdue Public Information Center loan documents.

On we loaned you the documents listed below.

They should have been returned by . Please return them immediately so that we can make then available to others. If you have already returned the documents or if there is some problem in this regard, please contact our interlibrary loan department as soon as possible at the address below or by calling (202)XXX-XXXX.

We appreciate your continuing cooperation in making our interlibrary loan service available to the public.

Sincerely,

Public Information Center
ATTN: Loan Department
P.O. Box 000
Washington, D.C. 20000

Public Information Center
Washington, D.C. 20000

Dear

On we mailed you a claim letter for the overdue document(s) listed below.

The document(s) were to be returned by . We have not heard from you or received those documents. If you have already returned them, or if there is a problem in this regard, please contact our interlibrary loan department at the address below or by calling (202)XXX-XXXX so that we may correct our records.

If we have not received the overdue document(s), or heard from you by , we will be forced to terminate interlibrary loan service to your organization/library. We hope for a speedy return of the document(s), or a reply from you so that we can continue interlibrary loan service to your organization.

Sincerely,

Public Information Center
ATTN: Loan Department
P.O. Box 000
Washington, D.C. 20000

ILL OVERDUES CLAIM FORM - INTERNAL

Customer's Name: Telephone: Lob Number:

RECORD OF CALLS AND CORRESPONDENCE

Call # 1: Date______ Spoke with customer ( ) Left message with ____________________
Customer will return call, date______ Call returned ( ) Call not returned ( )
Call # 2: Date______ Spoke with customer ( ) Left message with ____________________
Customer will return call, date______ Call returned ( ) Call not returned ( )
Call # 3: Date______ Spoke with customer ( ) Left message with ____________________
Customer will return call, date______ Call returned ( ) Call not returned ( )

NOTES

__Customer is out of town, will return, date______
__Customer has document ( ) Will return document to library, date______
__Customer says document was returned to: __________________________, date______
records checked ( ) Lending library called: Record cleared ( ) Record not cleared ( )
__Customer requests renewal ( ) Lending library grants ( ) Due date______ Renewal denied ( )
__Document is lost ( ) Lending library requests: Replacement copy ( ) Pay by check ( )
__Customer agreed to: Date______ Replace document ( ) Pay by check ( )
__ Library agreed to: Date______ Replace document ( ) Forms submitted Acquisitions ( )
Date______ Pay by check ( ) Forms submitted
__Other notes:

INTERLIBRARY LOAN STATISTICS

______ (YEAR)

MONTH	REQUESTS	FILLED	PREVIOUS REQUESTS FILLED	OTHER LIBRARY REQUESTS	FILLED	TOTAL REQUESTS	TOTAL FILLED	CONGRESS-IONALS RECEIVED	(ILL) XEROX	XEROX	TOTAL XEROX
JANUARY											
FEBRUARY											
MARCH											
APRIL											
MAY											
JUNE											
JULY											
AUGUST											
SEPTEMBER											
OCTOBER											
NOVEMBER											
DECEMBER											
TOTAL											

6

REFERENCE

Reference requests for which forms are generally used fall into three main categories: requests for information, requests for specific publications, and requests for which either the client or the librarian decides that an online search is necessary.

Forms to record a request for information, the search strategy used, and the information and/or publications provided, can give the library manager a valuable overview of the demands being made on the library's collection and staff. The information can guide acquisitions as well as serving as a guide to which offices within the organization are making the greatest use of the library's services. In the long run these forms can provide much more detailed, accurate, and measurable information than the impressions of the Reference Librarian about how the library is used. The forms also allow a considerably more in-depth analysis than the reference statistics forms, which tend to convey only numbers of requests rather than the difficulty or subject area. When filed by subject, these forms can also save a lot of time when the same subject is requested again, since ground previously covered in the search process need not be repeated.

Literature request forms make up another important category of forms used in the reference area. Most of these forms are designed to be completed, at least in part, by the requester. The most complete examples of these forms keep track of the request as it moves from the patron who initiated it, through the reference section where the publication may be retrieved for the user, or forwarded to be handled on interlibrary loan, or purchased for the library's collection by the acquisitions section. There is often a place to note the time frame within which all of this should take place and to record a final resolution of the request.

The online search request forms provide a record of the countless details which the librarian performing the search should have available in order to make the best use of online time. Many forms are designed to be completed either by the library patron or by the librarian during the reference interview. By following the guidelines on a carefully completed online search form, the librarian can perform a search which will yield citations most pertinent to the user's work and prove cost efficient as well.

6. Reference

A. Information Requests and Responses

B. Literature Requests

C. Database Searching

1. Search Requests
2. Search Transmittals and Evaluations
3. Search Logs and Statistics

D. Reference Statistics

Information Requests and Responses

RESEARCH IN LIBRARY

____
DATE

NAME ______________________

BUSINESS ______________________

SCHOOL ______________________

INFORMATION REQUESTED: ______________________

____

SOURCES USED:

FROM			RECEIVED BY	DATE OF REQUEST
BUILDING	ROOM	PHONE NO.	ANSWERED BY	NEEDED BY
QUESTION				
NOTES				
SOURCES CONSULTED				

Reference Request

Date Out:__________
Search Time:________

LIBRARY INQUIRY

____Telephone   ____Mail   ____In Person

RECEIVED BY ________________   DATE________________

REQUEST CLASSIFICATION

____Admin.
____Govt.Serv.
____Client
____Student
____Other

REQUEST BY:

NAME____________________
ADDRESS__________________
____
TELEPHONE________________
CLIENT___________________
CHARGE #_________________

REQUEST DESCRIPTION:

REPLY:

TYPE OF REQUEST:

____Ready Reference
____Extended Search
____In-House Publication
____Photocopying
____Messenger Dispatch

TYPE OF RESPONSE:

____Informational Answer
____Bibliography
____Ordered Material
____Collection Usage
____Inter-Library Loan
____Referral

M NM S A SUBJECT/CODE:____________________

NAME ____________________

TITLE ____________________

COMPANY ____________________

ADDRESS ____________________

____

____

PHONE (   ) ____________

QUESTION

RESPONSE

	DATE	BY
RECEIVED	/ /	
HANDLED	/ /	

DUE DATE____________________

RESPONSE: TYPE_____HOURS_____DAYS___

REFERENCE/RESEARCH REQUEST — Date Requested:

Name of Requester:	Date Required:	Office Symbols:	Extension:

Request:

Search History:

Type of Request:
☐ Telephone ☐ Letter ☐ In Person

Source of Request:
☐ CC ☐ C ☐ Federal
☐ CC:Regional/District ☐ C:Regional/District ☐ Private
Other: ☐ ____________

Request Completed:
Date: Letter Sent:

Source of Answer:
☐ IRS ☐ Federal Library ☐ Other

Nature of Request:
☐ Circulation ☐ Short Research (0-10 min.) ☐ Average Research (11-30 min.) ☐ Extended Research (31+ min.)

INQUIRY NO.	RECEIVED		DEADLINE		CALL BACK	RESEARCHER
	DATE	HOUR	DATE	HOUR		

SPECIAL INSTRUCTIONS

ADDRESS:

PHONE NUMBER:

REQUESTER CATEGORY

REQUESTER:

ASSIGNED TO:		
DIV	SEC	UNIT

MODE OF RECEIPT	RECEIVED BY	SUBJECT(S)		

MAJOR PROJECT NO.	NO. OF ITEMS REQUESTED	LAST NAME	RESEARCHER (PRINT)	INITIALS	DAYS	HOURS	MINUTES 1-15	16-30	31-45	46-59
			CLEARING REVIEWERS SEC							
			DIV							
			OTH							
			DO							

CLEARED DIVISION		TYPE	REFERENCE FORM(S)		
DATE	HOUR				

ASSISTANCE REQUESTS: /Information Services

Reference ( )
Program ( )

REQUESTOR:

Name: ____________________

Organization: ____________________

Address: ____________________

____

Phone: ( ) ____________________

SUBJECT REFERENCE: ____________________

DATE: ____________________

REQUEST: ____________________

____

____

____

ACTION TAKEN: ____________________

____

____

FOLLOW-UP: (Use Back of White Card)

STAFF: ____________________

REFERRED BY: ____________________

157 - 3-PART FORM

Public Information Service
Interesting Reference Questions
Month: ____________________

Please note the QUESTION, ANSWER, and SOURCE.

Staff

Non-Staff

REQUEST/RESPONSE RECORD	DATE RECEIVED	DATE COMPLETED
	PROCESSED BY	
REQUESTER (NAME AND TITLE)	TELEPHONE NO	
ORGANIZATION ACTIVITY		
ADDRESS		

REQUEST

ACTION TAKEN

_____ NEW COMPUTER SEARCH

_____ STANDARD PACKAGE

_____ UPDATED STANDARD PACKAGE

_____ WITHOUT COMPUTER SEARCH

_____ ACTIONS

_____ DISTRIBUTION DOCUMENTS

_____ XEROX DB ITEMS

_____ ABSTRACTS

REFERRED TO

NUMBER

RESPONSE

REFERENCE REQUEST FORM

Date: ______________________

Name: ______________________

Title: ______________________

Department: ______________________

Phone Number: ______________________

Date Needed by: ______________________

Date Completed: ______________________

(Please check one)

Walk-in _______
CEO _______
Phone _______
Inter-office _______
Public _______

Other Library _______

Cost Center _______

Location _______

Request:

Purpose: ______________________

Sources:

Database Search: ______________________

____

Inter Library Loan:

Messenger: ______________________

Comments: ______________________

____

Reference Request Form	Side 1

NAME ______________________ EXT. __________

SUBJECT AREA -- CHECK ONE

- ____ Communications
- ____ Corporation/Securities
- ____ Election Law
- ____ Environmental
- ____ Food & Drug
- ____ Government Contracts
- ____ Insurance
- ____ Intellectual Property
- ____ International Trade
- ____ Tax
- ____ Trade Regulation
- ____ Other, Specify __________

DATE AND TIME ______________________

CLIENT NAME AND MATTER ______________________

CLIENT NUMBER ______________________

DEADLINE DATE AND TIME ______________________

USE THE SPACE BELOW TO CLEARLY IDENTIFY THE NATURE OF YOUR REQUEST:

FOR STAFF USE ONLY	Side 2

IDENTIFY DATABASES AND DATABASE FILES USED IN COMPLETING THIS REQUEST.

BRS ____ D & B ____ DATATIMES ____ DIALOG ____

DOW JONES ____ LEXIS/NEXIS ____ NEWSNET ____

OCLC ____ VUTEXT ____ WASHINGTON ALERT ____

WESTLAW ____

USE THE SPACE BELOW TO DOCUMENT RESEARCH FOR THIS REQUEST. INCLUDING PERSONS CONTACTED, PHONE NUMBERS, PRINT SOURCES AND ANY ADDITIONAL COMMENTS.

Side 1

REFERENCE/RESEARCH REQUEST FORM

PLEASE COMPLETE ALL SECTIONS

Date of Request: ____________ Needed By: ____________
Requestor: ____________ Date
Division: ____________

Area of Interest/Research Topic: (If possible, please provide a brief statement on the use of this information. This may assist in determining research sources). ____________

This section must be completed before online information research is conducted. For assistance, please ask the Librarian.

Research Parameters:

____ Broad search, designed to retrieve as many relevant citations as possible, but which may retrieve irrelevant references.

Year(s) to be searched ____________

Limit search/U.S. sources only. ____ Yes ____ No.

Document Types: (Check all that apply)

___ Business Management Publications
___ Newspapers
___ Newsletters
___ Legal Publications
___ Books
___ Trade and Industry Publications
___ Technical Reports
___ Market Research
___ Government Documents

Article Types: (If applicable)

___ Analysis
___ Statistics
___ Background Information
___ News Items
___ Case Studies
___ Other: ____________

Printed Results Format:

___ Brief Title Description
___ Abstracts

Side 2

THIS SECTION TO BE COMPLETED BY INFORMATION RESOURCE CENTER STAFF ONLY

This request for information was received:

___ In Person
___ By Phone

___ Memo Letter
___ Proactive

ONLINE SEARCH

Keywords Used: ____________

Database System: ____________

Search Strategy: ____________

OTHER SOURCES USED

____

Date Completed: ____________

Request Completed By: ____________

Research & Reference Services

TAILORED INFORMATION PACKAGE REQUEST GUIDE

7/87

date request sent

date information required

staff requester

office

local telephone number

hours + or - DC time

ISN:

COMPL?

ENTRD?

(for R&RS use)

Please describe your subject in terms which define and limit the kind and amount of information you need for your present purpose. Mention any technical terms and synonyms we should look for, and any aspect of your subject that is not relevant in this situation. What useful information do you already have that we should not duplicate? (Continue on reverse if you need more space.)

Please check the types of sources you know you want searched.

☐ Subject literature ☐ Research organization(s) ☐ Individual expert(s)

☐ U.S. government ☐ Business firm(s) ☐ US or world press

☐ Other:

Name specific organizations or individuals we should start our search with, if known:

Language limits: ☐ English only ☐ other language(s) (specify):

Date limits: ☐ current year only ☐ past 3 years ☐ 1980-present ☐ 1970-present ☐ other:

Geographic limits:

Any other limits?

What kind of Tailored Information Package would you prefer? Our usual products are listed below, but, feel free to suggest something else.

- Reference Package (quick assembly of relevant citations, abstracts, or other reference information as appropriate)
- Document Package (selection of a few highly relevant items
- Diskette (downloaded sets of Development Information System records; specify format and send blank)
- Finished bibliography (compiled, selected, organized, and annotated according to your requirements)

LIBRARY

NAME	PHONE	ROOM	BUILDING

INITIAL
DATE

REQUEST:

MANUAL SOURCES USED:

1. ______ 3. ______ 5. ______

2. ______ 4. ______ 6. ______

COMPUTER SEARCH

Files:

1. ______ 2. ______ 3. ______ 4. ______ 5. ______ 6. ______

SEARCH WORDS / KEYWORDS:

1. ______ 4. ______ 7. ______

2. ______ 5. ______ 8. ______

3. ______ 6. ______ 9. ______

SEARCH STRATEGY:

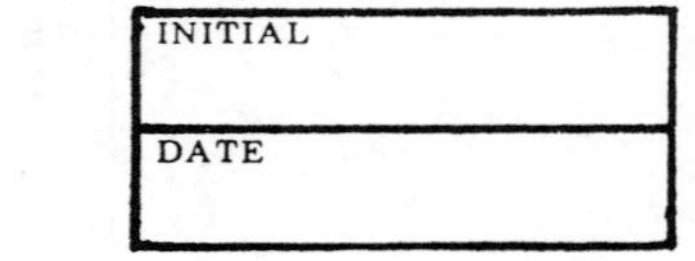
INITIAL

DATE

TO:

Date____________________

Subject File____________

Ref. #__________________

FROM:

RE: Your inquiry on________________________________

____ We enclose the following item(s):

____ Please return the materials marked "ON LOAN" within 3-4 weeks so we may serve other members.

____ We refer you to the following organization which has special expertise in the subject:

COMMENTS:

We hope these materials and suggestions will be helpful
is used to expedite service to members.

TO: DATE:

DEPT:

FROM:

Reference & Research Service
Headquarters Library EXT:

Your request for library service (attached) is returned to you for the following reasons.

____Justification or approval incorrect.

____Need to know missing/insufficient

____Author/Title is incomplete/incorrect

____Publisher address is incomplete/incorrect

____Report number is missing

____Contract number is missing

____Date of publication is missing

____Your reference is needed

TO:
FROM:
DATE:
RE: YOUR REQUEST FOR ______________________

I. STATUS OF SEARCH

*YOUR SEARCH HAS BEEN GIVEN TO THE LEGAL ASSISTANT DEPARTMENT (CALL)

COMPUTER DATABASES USED:
LEXIS WESTLAW NEXIS DIALOG D/J NEWS

SOURCES CONTACTED:

☐ PUBLISHER ______________________

☐ COURT ______________________

☐ AGENCY ______________________

☐ ASSOCIATION ______________________

☐ LAW LIBRARY ______________________

☐ DOCUMENT RETRIEVAL SERV. ______________________

☐ OTHER ______________________

II. DOCUMENT AVAILABILITY

THE DOCUMENT YOU REQUESTED:

☐ IS ATTACHED. DATE DUE: ______________________

☐ HAS BEEN ORDERED AND SHOULD ARRIVE ON ________ VIA ______________________

☐ IS AVAILABLE AT ______________________
MAY I ARRANGE AN APPOINTMENT?

☐ IS NOT AVAILABLE. I RECOMMEND THAT ______________________
____
____

PLEASE CALL ______________ AT EXT. ______
FOR MORE INFORMATION.

Literature Requests

PLEASE PRINT

R | M-Q | L | K | H-J | A-G

CALL NO.

AUTHOR

DO NOT USE

JOURNAL OR BOOK TITLE

VOL. OR ISSUE

YEAR COPY

BORROWER'S NAME (PRINT)

DO NOT USE

ROOM BLDG.

AGENCY PHONE

LIBRARY

S-V | Z | PERIOD | UNCL. | OTHER

PRESS FIRMLY PRESS FIRMLY PRESS FIRMLY

CALL NUMBER

AUTHOR ....

BOOK/PERIODICAL TITLE ....

....

....

PERIODICAL VOLUME OR DATE

Correct Legible Name and Address Required

STAFF USE ONLY

DESK NUMBER

NAME ....

ADDRESS ....

CITY ....

Not on Shelf

Clarify Call No.

Give Volume No.

Give Complete Date

Verify Call No.

Other Location (See Message)

Missing in Inventory

....

Date

If you have not indicated a desk number, do you wish this book for

Hold ☐ Overnight Call ☐

STAFF USE ONLY

Message ....

....

....

Last Name

Dk. Att. # ☐ CCF ☐

Author (Last name first)	Call Number
Title of Book or Periodical	

Place of Pub.	Publisher	Vol. & No.	Date

For library use:	Borrower's Name	Date
	Borrowed from:	
	Requested	Due
	Received	Returned

PERIODICALS

PRESS FIRMLY - WRITE ONLY ONE TITLE ON THIS SLIP
ALLOW 30 MINUTES FOR DELIVERY OF MATERIAL

Title of Publication ______________________

____

Issue(s) Wanted ______________________

____

SuDoc or UN Doc No. (if govt. pub) ______________________

DESK NUMBER

Name ______________________

Address ______________________

____

STAFF USE ONLY

Deck Att:

☐ Title not on shelf

☐ Issue(s) not on shelf

Latest on shelf

____

☐ On Loan Yes No

☐ Not bound

☐ Sent for binding on

____

Call No. ______________________

☐ Bound

☐ Title not received

☐ Issue(s) not received

NOTE: Your request will be expedited if complete information is furnished.				**FOR LIBRARY USE ONLY**	
TITLE OF BOOK/ARTICLE				CALL NO.	SOURCE
AUTHOR				RESPONSE	
TITLE OF PERIODICAL				CALL NO.	SOURCE
DATE	VOLUME(S)	PAGE(S)		RESPONSE	
REQUESTER'S NAME		DATE OF REQUEST		COMMENTS	
MAILING SYMBOL	BUILDING	ROOM NO.	TELEPHONE		
DATE NEEDED	SOURCE OF ABOVE REFERENCE ☐ INDEX MED ☐ CHEM ABSTR ☐ COMPUTER SEARCH ☐ OTHER *(Specify)*				
DELIVERY *(Check one)* ☐ CALL FOR PICKUP ☐ SEND BY MAIL					

LIBRARY DOCUMENT REQUEST

Parts 1 and 2 - LIBRARY
Part 3 - REQUESTER COPY

LITERATURE REQUEST

DATE ____________ INQUIRER ____________

INSTRUCTIONS:

____ Purchase Needed by ____________

____ Borrow Charge to ____________ Overhead

____ Photocopy

____ Quantity ____________ Client

REQUEST:

Author ____________

Title ____________

Publisher ____________ Date ____________ Price ____________

Source of Information ____________

For Journals ____________
(volume/date/pages)

DATE REQUEST COMPLETED ____________ INITIALS ____________

(Indicate Sources Searched on the Reverse)

LITERATURE REQUEST FORM

PROJECT NUMBER TO BE CHARGED:

Date: Name:

☐ Purchase

☐ Loan

☐ Retention copy

Needed by: ________ (Date)

Title/Subject of Publication: ________

Author(s):

Date Published:

Publisher:

Price:

For Journal: Volumes/Date:

LIBRARY REQUEST FORM

LIBRARY USE ONLY

Ordered: ________

Rec'd.: ________

O/P, O/S, N/A: ________

Search Time:

TO: Library

Date: ________

FROM: ________

# of copies: ________

________ Buy ________ Borrow

Client Name: ________

________ Photocopy ________ Obtain

Charge Number: ________

Author/Agency: ________

Title: ________

Publisher: ________
(or journal title, volume, pages, etc.)

Date of Publication: ________ Price: ________ N/Charge ________

Source of Information: ________ Telephone: ________

Notes: ________

LIBRARY REQUEST

Date ______________

☐ Regular ☐ Urgent

Request for: ☐ Purchase
☐ Loan
☐ Retention Copy

From: ______________ Room ______ Phone No. ______________

Author (s) ______________

Title ______________

____

Volume/Issue/Pages ______________ Publisher/Date ______________

Source of Information ______________ Client charge ______________

Information needed (use to request material when specific publications not known) ______________

____

____

Action taken:

Request taken by (Initials) ______________

Completed by (Initials) ______________ Date completed ______________

LIBRARY REQUEST FORM

☐ BORROW
☐ RESERVE
☐ PROCURE

☐ GEN'L BOOK COLL.
☐ CONG. DOCUMENT.

CALL NUMBER: ______________ BILL NO.: ______________

AUTHOR: ______________ COMMITTEE: ______________

TITLE: ______________

____

SOURCE OF REFERENCE: ______________

DATE OF PUBLICATION: ______________ PRICE: ______ PUBLISHER: ______________

FOR CONG. DOC./SUBJECT AREA: ______________

____

____

REQUESTOR'S NAME: ______________ DATE: ______________

LIBRARY ACTION: ______________

9-77

REQUEST FOR BOOK, PERIODICAL, OR INFORMATION ▶ NOTE – *USE SEPARATE SHEET FOR EACH TITLE*					1. Call number
2. Author or issuing agency					3. Type of material ☐ Publication ☐ Periodical ☐ Copy of article ☐ Microfiche ☐ Microfilm
4. Title of publication					
5. Volume	6. Number	7. Pages	8. Date	9. Publisher	
10. Title of periodical or author and title of article					
11. Source of reference					
12. Information needed *(Use to request material when specific publications not known)*					
13. Name of requester		14. Telephone number			15. Date of request
16. Name of division or agency		17. Building or address			18. Room number
19. Action taken					
20. Person referred to		21. Completed by – *Initials*	22. Reference code		23. Date completed

LIBRARY

REQUEST FOR INFORMATION

REQUESTOR'S NAME________________ TODAY'S DATE__________

OFFICE________________ NEEDED BY__________

TELEPHONE________________ DATE FILLED__________

- -

1. ITEM NEEDED:

Author (or periodical title, vol. and year)

Title (with author and pages for periodical articles)

Publisher

Year

Series name and number

Report number

- -

2. RESEARCH PROBLEM:

SOURCES CHECKED:

LIBRARY

REQUEST FOR BOOK, PERIODICAL, OR INFORMATION

LIBRARY USE ONLY

Dt. Ord.:__________

Dt. Recd.:__________

Search Time: 1-15 min.___ 15-30 min.___ 30-45 min.___ 45-60 min.___ Over 1 hr.___

Priority: ASAP___ Today___ 1-3 days___ 4-7 days___ Other___

Name of Requestor	Date
Address	Telephone

Requestor Classification

___Office of the President
___Insurance
___Finance
___Development
___General Counsel
___Public Affairs
___Treasurer
___Other

Action

Buy ___
Borrow ___
Order ___
Photocopy ___
Ready Reference ___
Extended Search ___
Messenger Dispatch ___
Collection Usage ___
Outside Source ___
Referral ___

Author or Issuing Agency

Title of Publication or Journal and Article Title

Volume	Number	Pages	Date	Publisher

Source of Information	Number of Copies	Price

Request Description

Reply/Action

JOURNAL SEARCH REQUEST

Title:
Author:
Call Number:

Patron's Name:
Phone:
Address:

Deadline:

Entered in CA Function by:

BOOK SEARCH REQUEST

Title:
Author:
Call Number:

Patron's Name:
Phone:
Address:

Deadline:

Entered in CA Function by:

PHOTOCOPY SERVICE REQUEST DATE ____________

REQUESTER ______________________________ EXT. ____________

DEPARTMENT ______________________ BUDGET/GRANT # ____________

OF COPIES ________ TOTAL PAGES ________ AMOUNT DUE ____________

I. JOURNAL TITLE ______________________________ VOL. # ________

ARTICLE TITLE ______________________________________

AUTHOR ______________________ MONTH/YEAR ________ PAGE ____ TO ____

II. BOOK TITLE ______________________________ EDITION/YEAR ________

AUTHOR ______________________ CALL # ________ PAGE ____ TO ____

NOTICE: WARNING CONCERNING COPYRIGHT RESTRICTIONS

The copyright law of the United States (Title 17, United States Code) governs the making of photocopies or other reproductions of copyrighted material.

Under certain conditions specified in the law, libraries and archives are authorized to furnish a photocopy or other reproduction. One of these specified conditions is that the photo copy or other reproduction is not to be "used for any purpose other than private study, scholar ship, or research." If a user makes a request for, or later uses, a photocopy or reproduction for purposes in excess of "fair use," that user may be liable for photocopy infringement.

This institution reserves the right to refuse to accept a copying order if, in its judgment, fulfillment of the order would involve violation of copyright law.

REQUEST FOR PHOTOCOPYING

Insert this slip in the book or journal. Be sure the heading is visible.

Leave it at the Reference Desk.

Name ____________________

Location ____________________

Please send ____________________

Will pick up ____________________

Journal title ____________________

Volume (Issue) ____________________

Pages ____________________

Book title ____________________

Author ____________________

Pages ____________________

Date ____________________

Deadline ____________________

Database Searching
Search Requests

DATABASE SEARCH REQUEST

SERVICE: ______________________________

*PLEASE BE AS SPECIFIC AS POSSIBLE!

DATE ______________

TIME ______________

INFORMATION NEEDED ______________________________

____

____

____

____

____

WHEN NEEDED? ______________________________

NAME AND EXTENSION ______________________________

****

FOR OPERATOR USE ONLY

1. LIBRARY ______________ FILE ______________

   SEARCH TERMS ______________________________

   ____

   ______________ # of HITS ______________

2. LIBRARY ______________ FILE ______________

   SEARCH TERMS ______________________________

   ____

   ______________ # of HITS ______________

3. LIBRARY ______________ FILE ______________

   SEARCH TERMS ______________________________

   ____

   ______________ # of HITS ______________

4. LIBRARY ______________ FILE ______________

   SEARCH TERMS ______________________________

   ____

   ______________ # of HITS ______________

5. LIBRARY ______________ FILE ______________

   SEARCH TERMS ______________________________

   ____

   ______________ # of HITS ______________

REFERENCE LIST	1	2	3	4	5
FULL TEXT	1	2	3	4	5
KWIC	1	2	3	4	5
________ VAR/KWIC	1	2	3	4	5

SEARCHER ______________ TIME COMPLETED ______________

QUICK BIBLIOGRAPHY REQUEST FORM

1) REQUESTOR´S NAME: ______________________________

2) REQUESTOR´S DIALOG USER NUMBER: ______________

3) QUICK BIBLIOGRAPHY TITLE: ____________________

____

4) SAVED SEARCH NUMBER ....

SET TO PRODUCE IN FILE 10 ....

NUMBER OF CITATIONS ....

SET TO PRODUCE IN FILE 110 ....

NUMBER OF CITATIONS ....

5) SAVED SEARCH NUMBER * ....

SET TO PRODUCE IN FILE 110 ....

NUMBER OF CITATIONS ....

* COMPLETE ITEM 5 WHEN SEPARATE SEARCHES
HAVE BEEN CREATED FOR FILES 10 AND 110.

6) DATE OF REQUEST: ______________________________

DATABASE SEARCH REQUEST

NAME		DATE	DATE REQUIRED
OFFICE	PHONE NUMBER	MAILCODE	NEED UPDATES?

SEARCH QUESTION

KEYWORDS: SYNONYMS AND RELATED TERMS

PUBLICATIONS TO BE RETRIEVED (Check as many as apply) : Books____ Journals _______
Articles______ Reports ______ Newspaper articles ______ Others ________
PERSONS ASSOCIATED WITH SUBJECT : ____________________
RELEVANT ORGANIZATIONS : ____________________
ANY TITLES ALREADY KNOWN : ____________________
LANGUAGE : English Only ______ Others ____________________
GEOGRAPHIC AREA TO BE COVERED : ____________________
YEARS TO BE SEARCHED : ____________________
PRINT OUT FORMAT : Citations only ______ Including Abstracts ____________
TYPE OF SEARCH (Check one) : Comprehensive with possible nonrelevant citations _________
OR Precise with fewer references____________

FOR LIBRARIAN'S USE

SEARCH STRATEGY (Indicate databases used and combination of terms)

LIBRARIAN'S NAME : FILING ELEMENT:

2/89

SEARCH REQUEST

NAME		REQUEST DATE	RESPONSE DATE
OFFICE/ORGANIZATION	PHONE NUMBER	MAILCODE	LIBRARIAN'S NAME

SEARCH REQUEST/KEYWORDS (Include synonyms and related terms)

How did you learn about the Database? ____________________

____

Reason for the request: ____________________

____

FOR LIBRARIAN'S USE

SEARCH STRATEGY

✓ DISCREPANCIES FOUND AND FEEDBACK TO DATABASE MANAGER DATE: ______

2/89

ONLINE SEARCH REQUEST FORM

RESEARCH LIBRARY

NAME________________________________DIVISION__________DATE_______________

PHONE____________STOP___________YOUR DEADLINE________________________

SEARCH TOPIC - In narrative form describe your search question using any known synonyms, acronyms, special or technical terms, or spelling variations you know about. Underline key words. Indicate any topics related to your problem which are not of interest to you.

TIME SPAN - Do you wish to limit this search to a particular time span (days, years, months)? Please specify.

LITERATURE - Do you wish to receive references to the following?

-Newspaper articles

-Working papers (economics)

-Journal articles - please specify banking journals, economic journals, business & finance journals, other?

LANGUAGE - Do you wish to retrieve references to English language documents only?

Date ____________ REQUEST FOR INFORMATION RETRIEVAL SERVICE ____________

Name ______________________________ Unit ____________

Phone number ______________ Room Number ______________

---

* PLEASE CHECK THE APPROPRIATE BOXES *

Type of Information	YES	NO
Engineering/Science	( )	( )
Statistics	( )	( )
Marketing	( )	( )
Economic Theory	( )	( )

Type Of Publications	YES	NO
Trade	( )	( )
Scholarly	( )	( )
Government	( )	( )
Legal; Congressional	( )	( )
Unpublished	( )	( )

Geographic Coverage	YES	NO
U.S.	( )	( )
Worldwide	( )	( )
Regional (Specify below)	( )	( )

Language	YES	NO
English only	( )	( )
Any	( )	( )

How Far fack in time should literature be searched? ______________

____

Format of Citations	YES	NO
Abstracts	( )	( )
Titles Only	( )	( )

************** SEARCH STATEMENT ***************

Please describe in your own words the topic to be searched. First, indicate the major concepts involved, including key terms. If pertinent, qualify further by the use of synonyms, acronyms, abbreviations, authors, government agencies and programs, industries, SIC codes, or company names.

Indicate any aspect of the subject which should not be included.

Search subject: ____________________
____

Diskette: _____ File Name: ________

COMPUTER SEARCH REQUEST

Please complete this form and send to   Library. If you have any questions, please call extension

Requester's name ______________________________ Date ____________

Department ______________________________ Date needed ______

Telephone number ______________________________ Bldg. ____________

Searcher's name ______________________________ Rm. No. __________

Description of the search topic. Include useful key words or phrases. Please be as specific as possible.

Other pertinent information (variant spellings, synonyms, scientific or technical terms):

Are they any words or terms that should be excluded?

Scope of search: _______ Comprehensive ___________________ Limited (please specify)

Type of information needed:

_____ All types   _____ Journal articles   _____ Books

_____ Newspaper articles   _____ Government documents   _____ Dissertations

_____ Other (please specify) ______________________________

Time period to be covered: _____ All years

_____ Other (please specify) ____________________

Language limitations: _____ English only _____ Other languages ______________

Format desired: _____ Bibliographic citation (author, title, journal, date)

_____ Abstracts (if available) _____ Full text (if available)

When search is completed: _____ Please send to my ATEX queue ______________

_____ Please call me and I will pick up

_____ Please send interoffice mail

REQUEST FOR BIBLIOGRAPHIC SEARCH

1. REQUESTORS NAME
2. PHONE NO.
3. SERVICE/SYMBOL
4. DATE REQUESTED
5. DATE NEEDED

6. FACILITY NAME ADDRESS

7. CHECK IF:
☐ STAFF ☐ STUDENT ☐ RESIDENT

8. CHECK ONE:
☐ WILL PICK UP
☐ PLEASE MAIL

9. SEARCH TOPIC: *Please provide a detailed statement in narrative form of your search topic. Be as specific as possible. State points to be excluded. Include synonyms which might help to describe your topic. Complete items 1-13.*

10. PURPOSE OF SEARCH
☐ PATIENT CARE
☐ RESEARCH
☐ EDUCATION
☐ PUBLICATIONS/PRESENTATION
☐ LIBRARY STAFF USE
☐ *(Specify)*

11. SUGGESTED DATA BASES
☐ MEDLINE
☐ PSYC INFO
☐ *(Specify)*

12. PREFERENCES
☐ VERY FEW RELEVENT ARTICLES
☐ COMPREHENSIVE, WITH POSSIBILITY OF PERIPHERAL MATERIALS

EXPECTED NUMBER OF CITATIONS ____________________

☐ BOOKS ☐ AUDIOVISUALS ☐ ABSTRACTS
☐ JOURNAL ARTICLES ☐ REVIEW ARTICLES

13. YEARS TO B INCLUDED:

14. LANGUAGE
☐ ENGLISH ☐ ALL ☐ *(Specify)*

15. CATEGORIES
☐ HUMAN ☐ FEMALE ☐ CHILD
☐ ANIMAL ☐ ADULT ☐ *(Specify)*
☐ MALE ☐ AGED ☐

16. SOURCES ALREADY SEARCHED/ OR CURRENT RELEVANT CITATIONS/ AUTHORITIES (LIST DATES WHEN APPLICABLE)

17. FACILITY LIBRARIAN REVIEWING REQUEST *(Signature)*

SEARCH ANALYST USE ONLY *(Use stamp to overprint if desired)*

ONLINE SEARCH REQUEST FORM - SUBJECT SEARCHES

Date______________________

Requestor______________________

Unit______________________

Phone__________ Room__________

Date /Time due______________________

I. Search Request - Describe what you are looking for in narrative form. Be sure to list any subject terms, synonyms, acronyms, or other terms which may help in searching the topic.

II. Search Parameters

☐ Broad search, designed to retrieve as many relevant citations as possible, but which may retrieve irrelevant references.

☐ Narrow search, which may retrieve fewer citations, but which also retrieves fewer irrelevant references.

Years to be searched ______________________ Number of items needed, if applicable______________________

Limit to U.S. sources only yes________ no________ Number of relevant items likely to be found, if known______________

TYPES OF MATERIALS REQUIRED (check all that apply)

☐ General business, management, personnel, labor periodicals ☐ Trade and industry periodicals ☐ Books
☐ News and popular periodicals ☐ Newspapers ☐ Computer periodicals and newspapers ☐ Govt docs.
☐ Technical reports ☐ Legal cases ☐ Law reviews ☐ Legal newspapers
☐ Laborlaw (identify subfile or "all")______________ ☐ other ______________

ARTICLE TYPES (if applicable)

☐ Case studies ☐ Surveys ☐ Statistics ☐ Overview or background information ☐ News items
☐ Other______________________

PRINT FORMATS (availability depends on database searched)

☐ Citations ☐ Citations with subject terms ☐ Citations with abstracts (not always available)
☐ Key-word-in-context format (not always available) ☐ Full-text

FORM OF OUTPUT ☐ Printout ☐ Download to: ☐ floppy disk
☐ Alpha-Micro
☐ ATEX: queue______________
Your file name______________

☐ LAN

CLIENT ID ______________________ **SEARCH LIMIT $**______________

ONLINE SEARCH REQUEST FORM - QUICK SEARCHES

Date__________________________

Requestor______________________

Unit__________________________

Phone__________Room__________

Date /Time due__________________

I. Search for a case cite

Case name

Court

Date of decision

II. Search for a previously identified article, news story, etc.

Title

Source

Publication date

CLIENT ID __________________________ **SEARCH LIMIT $**____________

ONLINE SEARCH REQUEST

Name	Ext.	Date requested	Date needed
Approval *(Signature)*		Div./Dept.	Project number

SUBJECT: *Give a narrative description. Be as specific as possible.*

KEYWORDS: *Acronyms, synonyms, spelling variations.*

NOTES: *Language, classification, limitations, document type, etc.*

SCOPE	DATE RANGE	FORMAT	PRINTS
☐ Comprehensive	☐ All	☐ Citation	☐ Under 25
☐ Limited	☐ Current year	☐ Abstract*	☐ 25-50
	☐ Other	☐ Full-text*	☐ All
	______ to______	(* if available)	

FOR USE OF LIBRARY/TECHNICAL INFORMATION CENTER

Files/Charges	Searcher	Date searched	Update
	Notes		

Search no.______

Date__________

ON-LINE SEARCH REQUEST FORM

Requestor____________________________ Bur./Div.__________ Phone __________

PLEASE FILL OUT ITEMS 1 - 3

1. Search topic: what subject(s) do you want searched? Be as specific as possible. Include synonyms and related terms. What kind of publications are you hoping to retrieve?

2. Do any of the items listed below suggest to you other information which might help us formulate a good comprehensive search? If so, please elaborate after each list.

   a. Special terms: jargon, popular names (of laws, reports, etc.), abbreviations.

   b. People and books: authors, persons associated with the subject, journal titles, book titles.

   c. Organizations: conferences, associations, foundations, schools, institutes, government agencies, international organizations, congressional committees.

   d. Commercial activities: industries, products, commodities, SIC numbers.

   e. Geographic areas: regions, countries, states, counties, cities, congressional districts.

3. Search limits

   a. Would you prefer: ___ a comprehensive search that retrieves most of the references relevant to your topic, but which may also retrieve many references not relevant?

   OR

   ___ a narrow search that may retrieve fewer references relevant to the topic, but which also retrieves fewer non-relevant references?

   b. English only ___ Other languages: ____________________

   c. Years to be searched ______________

   d. When is information needed? __________

   e. Preferred print-out format: ___citations only; ___abstracts or full-text

   f. Do you want a search update? ___Yes; ___No; ___send; ___pickup

****

Staff Use Only

Interviewer: Interview time(est.):

Reformulation of search topic:

Subject headings; thesaurus terms; LC classification (for LIBCON and post-73 CAIN)

Relevant data files/data base or file group (i.e. INFORM/Dialog; GEOREF/Orbit; USHOT/CASELAW/Juris)

<u>Plan for doing the search online</u>: straight subject search? thesaurus terms and phrases; alphabetical displays; truncations; full-text searching; combinations; other appropriate field searches; online or offline printing.

Time taken for strategy development:

<u>Results of search report</u>: indicate which techniques worked and what results were in terms of number of postings and relevancy of citations.

Need more space? Add another sheet.

CHECK THE FOLLOWING:

COMPUTER SEARCH REQUEST

Side 1

AFFILIATED:

Check one in each column:

___ Faculty
___ Fellow
___ Resident
___ Staff
___ Student
___ Alumni

___ Basic Science
___ Dental
___ Medical
___ Nursing
___ University

DATE:__________

REQUESTER: ______________________________ PHONE: __________
(please print)

DEPARTMENT:______________________________

BUDGET OR GRANT NUMBER:______________________________

AUTHORIZED SIGNATURE:______________________________

OR

ORGANIZATION:______________________________

LOCAL ADDRESS:______________________________

NON-AFFILIATED:

___ Other:

YEARS OF COVERAGE:

___ Latest 5 years
___ Latest 10 years
___ 1966 to present
___ Other:

PRINT FORMAT:

___ Author, title , source
___ With abstracts
___ Sort by: author
title
source

LANGUAGE:

___ All languages
___ English only
___ Other(s):

RESTRICT RESULTS TO:

___ Human
___ Animal
___ Male
___ Female
___ In vitro
___ Review
___ Infant, Newborn
___ Infant (1-23 mo.)
___ Child, Preschool (2-5)
___ Child (6-12)
___ Adolescence (13-18)
___ Adult (19-44)
___ Middle age (45-64)
___ Aged (65-79)
___ Aged, 80 and over

SEARCH TOPIC: Describe your search request in narrative form. Be specific and define terms that may have special meaning. Describe aspects *not* to be included. Indicate the purpose for which this search will by used, e.g., research, patient care, thesis.

Date needed by: __________.

KNOWN RELEVANT PAPER(S): Please supply full bibliographic citation for articles relevant to your request, published within the last three years. If no relevant papers have been found please state "none found".

SEARCH REQUIREMENTS:

_____ Broad search, designed to retrieve as many relevant citations as possible, but which might also retrieve many irrelevant references.

_____ Narrow search, designed to retrieve the most relevant references with few accompanying irrelevant references.

6/89

LIBRARY USE ONLY

Side 2

SEARCH FORMULATION:

Search Analyst:________________ Formulation time: ______________ Date Completed:________________

VENDOR	DATABASE(S)	CITATIONS		CONNECT		PAGES	
		ONLINE	OFFLINE	TIME	CHARGE	#	CHARGE
	TOTAL:						

METHOD OF PAYMENT:

CASH CHARGE INVOICE

Connect Time Charge $___________
Offline Citations ____________
Service Fees ____________
TOTAL $___________

Deposit received $___________
Date ____________
Initials ____________

COMPUTER SEARCH REQUEST

LIBRARY USE ONLY

Name *(Last, first)*		Date	ANALYST
Bureau/Institute/Division	Bldg./Room	Phone No.	DATE NEEDED BY
Position Title	Purpose of Search ☐ Patient Care ☐ Research ☐ Other:		
This Search is needed as part of my official duties	*Signature*		

1. Statement of subject to be searched *(including but not limited to significant words and phrases, chemical registry numbers, etc. If an author search, please supply full name, institutional affiliation and subject specialty.)*

2. Search delimiters

☐ All languages *or* ☐ English ☐ Other: ____________

☐ Human only

☐ Male only *or* ☐ Female only

☐ Animal only *or* ☐ Specific species: ____________

☐ Years to be searched ____________

3. List related articles or names of major contributors.

Author	*Journal Title*	*Volume, year, page nos.*

Library use only:

1. Date ran
Vendor ☐ N ☐ B ☐ D ☐
Database
Citations-on-line
Citations-off-line

2. Date ran
Vendor ☐ N ☐ B ☐ D ☐
Database
Citations-on-line
Citations-off-line

3. Date ran
Vendor ☐ N ☐ B ☐ D ☐
Database
Citations-on-line
Citations off-line

4. Date ran
Vendor ☐ N ☐ B ☐ D ☐
Database
Citations on-line
Citations off-line

ON-LINE RESEARCH REQUEST RECORD

Requester ______________________ Date ______________________

Dept. ______________ Tel. Ext. ______________ Mail Stop ______________

Project No.: ____________

1. Information required. Be as specific as possible, including points NOT to be searched.

2. Other restrictions (Time span to cover; language, etc.)

3. Sources already checked.

Approval ______________________ Project no. ______________________

Project leader, Department Head or Associate

.... Library Record ....

Strategy/Notes

Time spent on search ______________________ By Searcher ______________________

System(s)	Data Base(s)	Time: Start	Time: Finish	Print/Hits	Cost: Est.	Cost: Billed

WHITE COPY TO BE SIGNED BY APPROVING OFFICER; RETURNED TO LIBRARY.

YELLOW COPY—HELD IN LIBRARY

Date Rec'd: ____________
Date Ran: ____________
Computer Time: ____________
Off-Lines: ____________

SEARCH REQUEST

Name: ______________________ Dept.: ______________ Ext.: ________

Give a detailed statement of your requirements. (Describe subject matter for which search is to be conducted. Define terms that have special meaning in your request. Do not give simply a list of keywords.)

List any known relevant articles published in the last two years:

Indicate if you wish your search to be limited by any factor, such as publication year or date:

Indicate preference:

☐ Few, very relevant citations ☐ Comprehensive search with possibility of peripheral citations

Listed below are the major data bases (except MEDLINE) which are available. Please indicate those you wish to be searched. If you do not give a preference, the searcher will chose those most appropriate for your subject. See the Library staff for the availability of other data bases.

☐ BIOSIS PREVIEWS (Biological Abstracts) 1970-
☐ CA CONDENSATES (Chemical Abstracts) 1970-
☐ CHEMLINE (chemical synonyms) current
☐ DISSERTATION ABSTRACTS 1861-
☐ INSPEC (physics, engineering, computer sciences) 1969-
☐ NTIS (unclassified government reports) 1970-
☐ PSYCHINFO (Psychological Abstracts) 1967-
☐ TOXLINE (toxicology, pharmacology) 1966, 1972-

Please check here ☐ if you wish to be present when the search is conducted and you will be contacted regarding a suitable time.

ONLINE SEARCH REQUEST FORM

Name of Requestor________________ Date________________________
Telephone Number__________________ Date needed________________
Charge to Dept. #________________

1. Title of search request_____________________________________

2. Description: Describe the subject/topic of your request in a few concise sentences. Are you looking for a particular item or as much information as possible on this subject?____

____

____

3. Keywords: List key terms or phrases that describe the topic. Include scientific or technical terms as well as common terminology. List synonyms and popular phrases.____

____

4. List related topics that you are not interested in.________________

____

5. List authors that write on this subject. Are you interested in finding more items by these authors?____

____

6. Journals: List journals that have or may have articles on your subject.

____

7. Publication years: _____All available. Nothing before______,after_______.

8. Citation: List a citation for an article relevant to the subject/title request.

____

____

9. Language: English only______Other______

10. Document type: Books_____Journals______Other______

11. Maximum amount to be spent_________________________________

12. If you could find the perfect article, what would its title be? __________

____

13. Please list any other information that will be useful for this online search.

Side 1

ON-LINE BIBLIOGRAPHIC SEARCH FORM

NAME ______________________ SEARCH NO. ______________________

DEPARTMENT ______________________ NO. ______ PHONE NO. ______

PROJECT NO. ______________________ DATE ______________________

__ Mail the search to me START TIME __________ END TIME __________

__ Call me and I'll pick up PROJECT NUMBER ______________________

DEFINING THE SEARCH

Search Topic - Describe the subject on which you are seeking information. Include alternate names and names of descriptive terms for specific methods or techniques that apply to this topic.

____

____

____

____

List important terms (words or phrases) and any synonyms or related terms that you wish to include or exclude. Include both scientific and common terms. Please explain terms and use as much detail as necessary. Attach a second sheet if necessary.

TERMS TO SEARCH	SYNONYMS	EXCLUDED TERMS

Include authors or organizations whose work is of interest, listing all names as completely as possible. Please indicate if you wish to exclude documents by any authors or organizations because of prior familiarity with their publications.

____

____

____

____

____

____

If possible, list two or three recent references that relate to this search. (This will greatly facilitate searching and enhance relevance of search results to your needs.) Attach copies if you have them.

____

____

____

Side 2

LIMITING OR QUALIFYING THE SEARCH

What type of search do you need? (Check all applicable)

______ RETROSPECTIVE - looking back over the available years of the database

______ CURRENT AWARENESS - last year or two

______ BROAD - a fairly long list, missing few relevant references but probably including many non-relevant items

(EXAMPLE)

LANUGAGE:_____ENGLISH ONLY_____ANY LANGUAGE_____OTHER(Specify)_____

______ NARROW - a relatively short list containing mostly relevant items with the possibility that some relevant items will be missed

DATES: What is the earliest date that references will be useful to you?

____

(References from some databases may go back to 1964 or 1966)

OTHER RESTRICTIONS OR LIMITATIONS ______________________

____

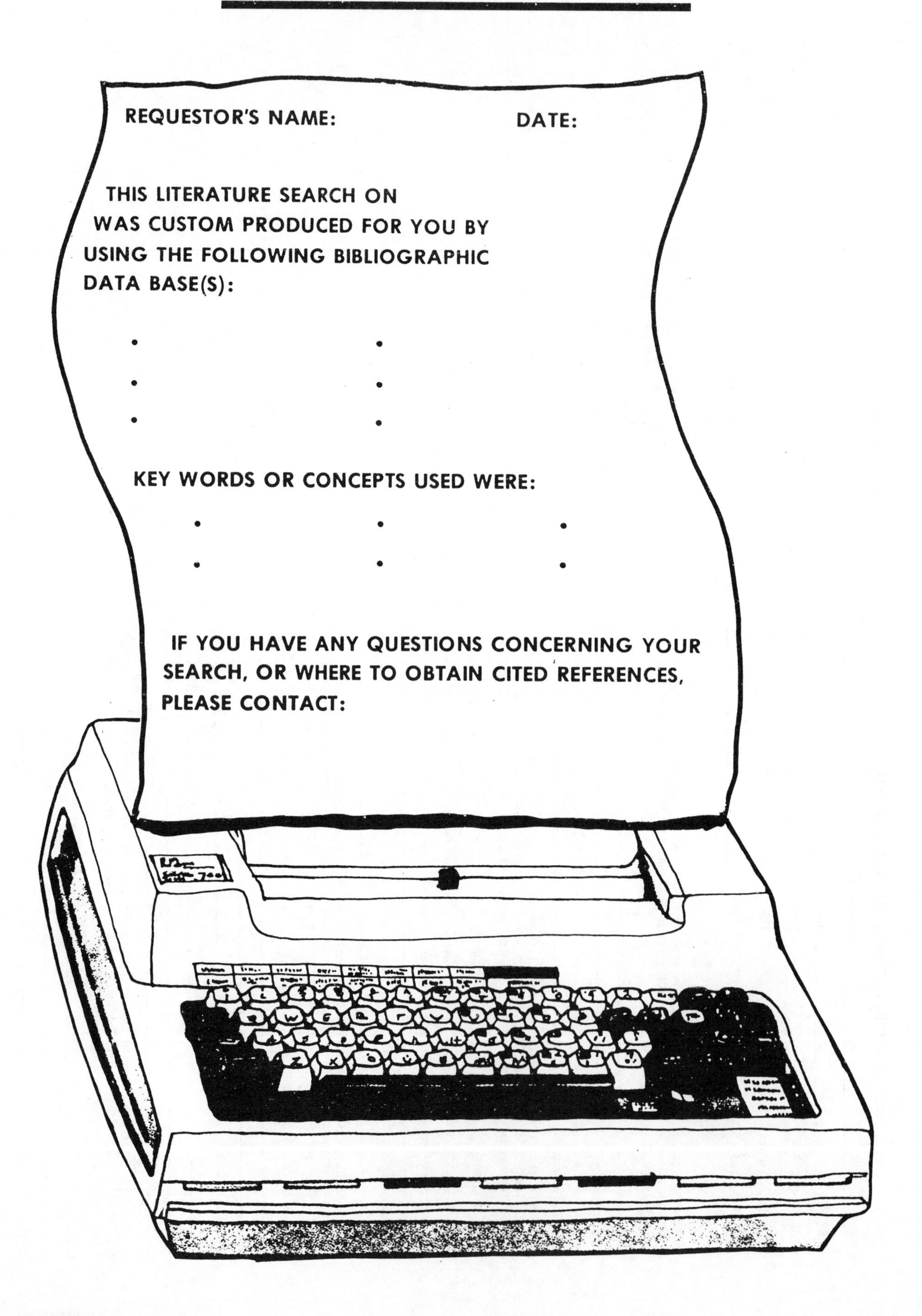

REQUESTOR'S NAME: DATE:

THIS LITERATURE SEARCH ON
WAS CUSTOM PRODUCED FOR YOU BY
USING THE FOLLOWING BIBLIOGRAPHIC
DATA BASE(S):

-
-
-
-
-
-

KEY WORDS OR CONCEPTS USED WERE:

-
-
-
-
-
-

IF YOU HAVE ANY QUESTIONS CONCERNING YOUR
SEARCH, OR WHERE TO OBTAIN CITED REFERENCES,
PLEASE CONTACT:

To: Date:

Department: Ext.:

From: Reference & Information Center

Attached are the results of a database search you requested on the topic(s):

This search was prepared for you by:

If you have any questions about the results of the search or need additional searches, please contact us.

Database searched: Time period covered:

The documents listed in this search can be obtained for staff members by the Reference & Information Center. Please inquire about our document delivery services.

ONLINE LITERATURE SEARCH

DATE: ______________

FOR: ______________________________________

PHONE: ________________ MAILCODE: __________

SUBJECT: ___________________________________

____

DATABASES SEARCHED: _________________________

____

IF YOU HAVE ANY QUESTIONS REGARDING THIS SEARCH, PLEASE CONTACT:

____

PHONE:

An online search evaluation form is attached. Please fill out and leave the form at the Library or drop it in the interoffice mail

The Headquarters Library may have some of the books, reports or articles cited in your search result.

Reports and articles on microfiche are available for citations from the following DIALOG databases:

- **NTIS** (File 6) - all reports distributed by NTIS
- **ENVIROLINE** (File 40)- Environmental topics
- **CIS** (File 101) - Congressional hearings and reports

To locate materials cited from other databases:

1. For books and reports - check the **Catalog** on microfiche or ask a librarian to search the Online Catalog.

2. For periodical articles check the **Journal Holdings Report**.

Items not available in the library may be requested through Interlibrary Loan. Request forms are available at the Circulation Desk.

DATE ____________________

REQUESTOR ____________________

COMMENTS ____________________

____

____

____

____

____

____

SEARCHER ____________________

Questions? Call the Reference Desk

DATE ____________________

REQUESTOR ____________________

COMMENTS ____________________

____

____

____

____

____

____

SEARCHER ____________________

Questions? Call the Reference Desk

DATE ____________________

REQUESTOR ____________________

COMMENTS ____________________

____

____

____

____

____

____

SEARCHER ____________________

Questions? Call the Reference Desk

DATE ____________________

REQUESTOR ____________________

COMMENTS ____________________

____

____

____

____

____

____

SEARCHER ____________________

Questions? Call the Reference Desk,

SEARCH EVALUATION FORM

REQUESTER'S NAME ______________________ DATE__________

SEARCH TOPIC____

____

NUMBER OF CITATIONS FOUND_________________________

HOW DO YOU RANK YOUR SEARCH? Good ☐ Fair ☐ Poor ☐

COMMENTS: ____

____

____

WERE NYT DATA BASE NOT AVAILABLE, WHAT SOURCES WOULD YOU HAVE USED AND HOW LONG WOULD IT HAVE TAKEN? ________

____

____

LIBRARY

Library

LITERATURE SEARCH RESULTS

Name:

Date:

Project:

Subject:

Computer Search Evaluation

Please take a few minutes to answer the following questions to help us improve our service. Feel free to make comments!

1. Were you satisfied with the results of the search?

   YES_______ NO_______

2. Was the search useful either in providing information or indicating that there was none?

   YES_______ NO_______

3. What percent of the retrieved documents would you consider relevant?

   ________%

4. Were the results of the search

   Too numerous ?_______ Not sufficient ?_____ Sufficient ?______

5. Would you avail yourself of this service again?

   YES_______ NO_______

6. If the computer search were not available, would you have done a manual search?

   YES_______ NO_______

7. Estimate time saved by having this search run.

   1 - 3 hours ____ 10 - 12 hours _____

   4 - 6 hours ____ 13 + hours _____

   7 - 9 hours ____ manual search impossible _____

8. Did you receive adequate information and assistance from the Library staff when you requested the search and/or were given the results?

   YES_______ NO_______

Name ______________________ Bureau/Div.____________________

Date______________________

Comments:

Please return the completed form to:

TECHNICAL INFORMATION SERVICES

- -

TO: ROOM:

Attached are the results of an on-line search done for

you on ______________________, with the title ________

____.

Your comments on this product and/or the services of TIS would be appreciated.

RELEVANCE: ____________ of the _____ citations were relevant to my needs. I requested _______ of the cited documents.

NEW INFORMATION: _______ were not previously known to me.

SERENDIPITY: _______ were useful to me for other needs.

TIME: _____min._____hrs. spent explaining information requirements.

_____min._____hrs. spent participating in the On-line search.

COMMENTS

To request any of the cited items, please submit Library Information Request for each title.

Please fold up to the dotted line and staple and return.

THANK YOU

COMPUTER SEARCH SERVICE

TO:______________________________ DEPARTMENT:_____________________________________

FROM:____________________________ DATE:____

The results of the computer search you requested are attached. We have marked those citations that are available in the Library. If there is an important book or article that you need to see that is not available in our library, you might wish to contact our Interlibrary Loan department at ext. . Please indicate that your request is the result of an online search.

If you wish to discuss your search or explore other aspects of it in another search, please give us a call at extension .

Notes:

****

In order to evaluate and improve the Library's Computer Search Service, we would appreciate your taking the time to answer the questions below and return this form to the Library. We welcome any comments and suggestions that you may have.

Search Topic:__________________________ Project:_______________________________

How did you learn about the Computer Search Service?____________________________

____

Were the citations received relevant? ______Yes ______No

Comments:____

Were the citations new to you?

______All ______Most ______Some ______None

Was the delivery time reasonable? ______Yes ______No

Are you satisfied with the comprehensiveness of the search?______Yes ______No

Is there any way we can improve this service to better fit your needs?

Please return this form to

LIBRARY SEARCH COSTS FORM

________________ ________________ ________________

Requestor *Client ID* *Date*

Date	Database or file or system	Estimated cost	Logon time @ rate	Search units @ unit price	Print units @ unit price	Totals

ONLINE SEARCHING LOG

DAY ____________________

DATE ____________________

LOGON	LOGOFF	TOTAL TIME	VENDOR	DATABASE	SEARCHER	REQUESTOR	REMARKS/PROBLEMS

SEARCH LOG

DATE	SEARCHER	REQUESTER	DIVISION	SUBJECT OF SEARCH	VENDOR & DATABASE	TIME ONLINE	OFFLINE PRINTS	TOTAL COST	NOTES

Search No.	Date	Requestor & Phone No.	Agency	User	Subject Topic, Notes & Saves	Dia-log	Or-bit	NYT		File #/Name	Time	Line	Off-line	Date Rec.d.	Bill Done

Reference Statistics

Reference & Information Center
Public Services Statistics

	In person	Telephone	Letter	Ready Reference	Research	Req. for company prods. & publications
Administrative Svcs.						
Banking Group						
Communications Group						
Comptroller						
Education Group						
General Counsel						
Government Relations						
Other						
Public & Students						
Industry						
Clients						
Libraries						
Other						
Media Contacts						
Totals						

LIBRARY REFERENCE STATISTICS

For the month ____________

I. Interlibrary Loan

Number of Loans Borrowed (non-owned items) ____________

Number of Loans Borrowed (owned, but missing) ____________

Total Loans Borrowed ____________

Average Cost per Loan ____________

Total Cost of All Loans for the Month ____________

Number of Loans Loaned ____________

II. Computerized Information Retrieval

Database	Total Cost	Total Time HH/MM/SS	Total # Searches
Aviation Aerospace Online			
Berry Best			
Datatimes			
Dialog			
Dow Jones			
Dun & Bradstreet			
Legislate			
LEXIS/NEXIS			
Newsnet			
Nora			
OCLC			
Statenet			
Vutext			
Washington Alert			
Westlaw			

III. Reference Requests

Number of Reference Requests Completed ____________

Number of Information Requests Completed ____________

REFERENCE DESK TRANSACTIONS

WEEK:

REQUESTERS	Type of activity		8:30-10:30	10:30-12:30	12:30-2:30	2:30-4:30
Staff	Directional					
	Type 1 reference					
	Type 2 reference					
	Online Search					
	CD-ROM Search					
	OCLC Search					
	ISIS Search					
	Pubs.	# Distri.				
		# Requests				
Non-Staff	Directional					
	Type 1 reference					
	Type 2 reference					
	Online Search					
	CD-ROM Search					
	OCLC Search					
	ISIS Search					
	Pubs.	# Distri.				
		# Requests				

Record only transactions completed while on the Desk.
Include referrals under appropriated category; e.g., walk-ups Type 1.
Type 1 reference is a instructional/ready reference response--up to 15 minutes.
Type 2 reference is a search from 15 minutes to 1 hour.

REFERENCE WEEKLY STATISTICS

Name of Librarian:

Week of:

	Monday	Tuesday	Wednesday	Thursday	Friday	Total
Telephone Directional (library hours, regulations)						
Reference (ready reference and research information)						
In Library Reference (ready reference and research information including correspondence)						
Referrals						

Name ____________

Date ____________

PUBLIC SERVICES SECTION

Information Transactions

	REFERENCE												Holdings or Directional Questions	Problems/Remarks
	Bureau		Outside					Inquiry Method						
			Libraries		Other Users									
	Census Material	Other	Census	Other	Census	Other	Total	Telephone	Visits	Corres.	Total			
Total														
Code	VII 1	VII 2	VII 4	VII 5	VII 7	VII 8	VII 10	VII 11	VII 12	VII 13	VII 14		VII 15	

DAILY REQUEST LOG

DATE:

							phone in
							walk in
							patron
							visitor?
							dept.
							request
							direct'l
							intermed
							research
							folders
							clips
							copies
							browse
							telephone
							archives
							out
							referred to
							search
							unanswered

Reference Desk Daily Log for ______________________

Walk-in	Phone	NAME & AFFILIATION	Non-Staff?	TIME GIVEN D	TIME GIVEN I	TIME GIVEN R	INFORMATION REQUESTED	SOURCE USED & ANSWER	REFERRED TO	Unanswered?

PAGE TALLY:

	W-I	P	D	I	R
Staff:					
Non-Staff:					

LIBRARY VISITORS:

Staff:
Non-Staff:

RESEARCH SERVICES DIVISION STATISTICS

Branch Fiscal Year Month Total

I. CIRCULATION TRANSACTIONS

A. REQUESTS RECEIVED
1. from Individuals ________
2. from Other branch libraries ________
3. from Outside Libraries ________

B. REQUESTS SENT
1. to Other branches ________
2. to LC (ALA form) ________
3. to Outside Libraries (ALA form) ________
4. to Outside Libraries (OCLC ILL) ________
5. to Document Delivery ________

C. LIBRARY LOAN ACTIVITY
1. Branch Volumes Circulated
a) to Individuals ________
b) to Other branches ________
c) to Outside Libraries ________

2. Branch Items Photocopied
a) for Individuals ________
b) for Other branches ________
c) for Outside Libraries ________

3. Volumes Received
a) from Other branches ________
b) from LC ________
c) from Outside Libraries ________

4. Photocopies Received (Items)
a) from Other branches ________
b) from LC ________
c) from Outside Libraries ________
d) from Document Delivery ________

5. Overdue Notices Sent ________

II. REFERENCE ACTIVITY

A. Questions under 5 minutes ________
B. Questions over 5 minutes ________
C. Electronic Searches ________
D. Letter responses ________

II. OTHER ACTIVITY (Please Specify)
A.________ ________
B.________ ________
C.________ ________

REQUESTS FOR INFORMATION

DATE	REQUESTOR	DEPT.	SUBJECT / SOURCE	ANSWER	
				Y	N

KK/588

PERIODICALS CONTROL

Periodicals and serials, with their frequency and variation in publication, pose special problems in designing forms to monitor their progress through the library's system. Forms must be able to handle weeklies and annuals, titles renewed yearly and those renewed every three years, journals to be routed and those to be shelved, as well as other local variations.

There are a variety of periodical check-in and order forms available from library supply companies that are used by many libraries. Many examples can be examined in the dealers' catalogs. The examples of check-in and order forms designed in-house show how some libraries accommodate their particular recording needs.

Claims for periodical issues never received are a continuing responsibility. Consequently, most libraries are well-advised to handle them with a form letter, which only needs to have the pertinent information filled in. Librarians may want to have separate form letters to deal with claims to different suppliers, or to handle paid subscriptions differently than titles received without charge.

Statistics on periodical orders are usually included on acquisitions statistics forms while circulation and routing statistics are ordinarily handled as a part of circulation.

7. Periodicals Control

A. Periodical and Serial Records

1. Data Entry
2. Check-in

B. Periodical Order Records, Renewals, and Evaluations

C. Periodical Claims

D. Routing Forms

Periodical and Serial Records
1. Data Entry
2. Check-in

INMAGIC DATA ENTRY FORM FOR SERIALS

TITLE RECORDS

DOES A TITLE/SUPPLIER RECORD ALREADY EXIST?

ID (10 characters or fewer, upper case):_ _ _ _ _ _ _ _ _ _
DOCNO (publisher's):____________________
TITLE (TI) initial caps, no leading articles, organization name 1st:____________________
Subtitle (STI):____________________
EDITION (ED) ex: Japanese edition:____________________
SUBJ (DE) FMI field in words:____________________
LOCN (circle): AR B CB F FMI I L QR S ST CH DE LA *

ORDER (ORD) supplier's order number:____________________
ORDERDT (ODT) day-month-year:____________________
CHECKNO:____________________
ACCT (of requesting department):____________________
DEPT (requesting) circle: AD CM CA CV ED GR IS LP MB OS OSDC OSDE OSCH OSLA RS ST TS OU
PRICE (annual, don't use $ sign): _ _ _ . _ _
TYPE (TP) circle: JR NL NP VD

FREQ (circle): D W BW SM M BM Q SA A Irregular
Special____________________
START (check): on order issue date (day-mon.-yr.)____________________
EXPIRES (EXP) day-mon.-yr.:____________________
RENEW (REN) usu. 2 mon. before expires, day-mon.-yr.:____________________
HOLDINGS (HO) circle: year ______-______ number ______ *

SPECIAL (SPEC) ex: buyer's guide, index, etc.:____________________
DISPOSITION (DISP) circle: AB B C S T

SUPPLIER (SUP) full name:____________________
STATE (if is a state pub., full name):____________________
NOTES (NTS):

PROBLEM (PROB):

ISSN:____________________
PLACE (city or city & state of publisher):____________________
PUBLISHER (PUB):____________________
PUBADD (street f10, city, state, zip f10, country if appl.)

BINDERY (BIND) date sent:____________________
DATEIN (record entered):____________________
COPIES (CPS) # ordered:____________________
NUMBER (NUMB) # received:____________________

Do you need a supplier record?

Routing: No Yes:

INMAGIC DATA ENTRY FORM FOR SERIALS

SUPPLIER RECORDS

Check to see that supplier is not already in database.

ID (check list for latest number):_ _ _ _ _ _ _ _ _ _

ORDER (ORD) supplier's order number:______________________________

ORDERDT (day-mon.-yr.):__________________

SUPPLIER (SUP) full name:____

SUPADD (street f10, city, state, zip f10, country if appl.)

SUPTEL (area/num-bers):______/______-______

CONTACT:_________________________________

NOTES:

DATEIN (record entered):___________________

Doc. # 1040I

PERIODICAL DATA ENTRY

Function: c a d

Title____

Record ID________________ Holdings__________________

Subject__________________ Fre ____________________

Note__________ Pub ______________ Exp _____________

Paid Date _______ Cost ________ Route: Y N

Online serial check-in screen with sample record

```
Title[1]                                                              NoC
   Routedto
TITLE:  Title[1]
        Title[2]
FREQUENCY:  Frequency
'89  1 2 3 4 5 6 7 8 9 10 1 2 3 4 5 6 7 8 9 20 1 2 3 4 5 6 7 8 9 30 1
JAN  Jan
FEB  Feb
MAR  Mar
APR  Apr
MAY  May
JUN  Jun
JUL  Jul
AUG  Aug
SEP  Sep
OCT  Oct
NOV  Nov
DEC  Dec

ROUTEDTO: Routedto
LOCATION:  Location
PUBLISHER:  Publisher[1]
            Publisher[2]
BEGINNING DATE1   Beginning1          ENDING DATE 1  Ending1
VOL:   Vol
EXPIRATIONDATE1
COST:  Cost                            CHARGE:  Charge
NOTE:  Note[1]
       Note[2]
OCLC:  OCLC                             ISSN:  ISSN
```

```
TITLE:  Case Western Reserve Journal of International Law    c

FREQUENCY:  3 issues/yr
'89  1 2 3 4 5 6 7 8 9 10 1 2 3 4 5 6 7 8 9 20 1 2 3 4 5 6 7 8 9 30 1
JAN  Winter 89
FEB
MAR
APR
MAY
JUN
JUL
AUG
SEP
OCT
NOV
DEC

ROUTEDTO:
LOCATION:  FL
PUBLISHER:  Case Western Reserve School of Law

BEGINNING DATE1   Jan 79              ENDING DATE 1
VOL:   11-

COST:  16.00                          CHARGE:  5621-001
NOTE:

OCLC:  1553466                          ISSN:  0008-7254
```

Manual Check-in

NO. OF SUBSCRIPTIONS: ____________ DEPOS NO. ____________ CARD NO. ____________

YEAR	VOL.	JAN.	FEB.	MAR.	APR.	MAY	JUNE	JULY	AUG.	SEPT.	OCT.	NOV.	DEC.	INDEX
		1												
		2												
		3												
		4												
		5												

ISSUING BODY: ____________

FORMAT: ____________ FREQ: ____________

SEND TO: ____________ NEEDS ISSUES PULLED: ____________

KEY TITLE: LOCATION:

203A SIDE 1

KEY TITLE: ____________ OCLC NO. ____________

PUBLISHER: ____________

ADDRESS: ____________

CITY: ____________

CLAIM FROM: ____________ ____________

P.O. NO. ____________ PRICE: ____________

INVOICE NO. ____________ SUBN TERM: ____________

RETENTION PERIOD: ____________

NOTES:

203B SIDE 2

NO. OF SUBSCRIPTIONS: ______ DEPOS NO. ______ CARD NO. ______

Nos: 1- 00.

1	11	21	31	41	51	61	71	81	91
2	12	22	32	42	52	62	72	82	92
3	13	23	33	43	53	63	73	83	93
4	14	24	34	44	54	64	74	84	94
5	15	25	35	45	55	65	75	85	95
6	16	26	36	46	56	66	76	86	96
7	17	27	37	47	57	67	77	87	97
8	18	28	38	48	58	68	78	88	98
9	19	29	39	49	59	69	79	89	99
10	20	30	40	50	60	70	80	90	00

ISSUING BODY: ______

FORMAT: ______ FREQ: ______

SEND TO: ______ NEEDS ISSUES PULLED: ______

KEY TITLE: LOCATION:

204A SIDE 1

KEY TITLE: ______ OCLC NO. ______

PUBLISHER: ______

ADDRESS: ______

CITY: ______

CLAIM FROM: ______ ______

P.O. NO. ______ PRICE: ______

INVOICE NO. ______ SUBN TERM: ______

RETENTION PERIOD: ______

NOTES:

204B SIDE 2

NO. OF SUBSCRIPTIONS: ______ DEPOS NO. ______ CARD NO. ______

		1	2	3	4	5	6	7	8	9	10	11	12	13	14	15	16	17	18	19	20	21	22	23	24	25	26	27	28	29	30	31
YR	JAN																															
	FEB																															
	MAR																															
	APR																															
VO	MAY																															
	JUN																															
	JUL																															
	AUG																															
IN	SEP																															
	OCT																															
	NOV																															
	DEC																															

ISSUING BODY: ______

FORMAT: ______ FREQ: ______

SEND TO: ______ NEEDS ISSUES PULLED: ______

KEY TITLE: LOCATION:

205A SIDE 1

KEY TITLE: ______ OCLC NO. ______

PUBLISHER: ______

ADDRESS: ______

CITY: ______

CLAIM FROM: ______ ______

P.O. NO. ______ PRICE: ______

INVOICE NO. ______ SUBN TERM: ______

RETENTION PERIOD: ______

NOTES:

205B SIDE 2

PERMANENT VOLUMES: BOUND ________ MICROFORM ________

VOL & DATE	DATE SENT	DATE RECD	VOL & DATE	DATE SENT	DATE RECD	VOL & DATE	DATE SENT	DATE RECD

206A SIDE 1

SOURCE OF PERMANENT VOLUMES: ________

ADDRESS: ________

CITY: ________

INDEX NOTE: ________

____

SPECIAL INSTRUCTIONS: ________

____

BOUND VOLUMES:

COLOR: ________ COLOR CODE: ________

DATE DUE TO BE SENT TO BINDERY: ________

MAX. WIDTH OF VOL: ________ VOL. PER YR: ________

MICROFORM:

TYPE: ________

206B SIDE 2

PERIODICAL CHECK CARD

TITLE

W ______ SM ______ M ______ BW ______ Q ______ OTH ______

DATE OF PERIODICAL	RECEIVED	ROUTED	RETURNED	DATE OF PERIODICAL	RECEIVED	ROUTED	RETURNED

PERIODICAL ROUTING CARD

PUBLISHER

ADDRESS

☐ SUBSCRIPTION

☐ FREE

☐ EXCHANGE

ROUTING

NEW SUBSCRIPTION DATA SHEET

TITLE ____________________

____

TITLE NUMBER ____________________

SOURCE CODE ____________________

REQUESTOR ____________________

DEPARTMENT ____________________ PROJECT CHARGE ____________________

FREQUENCY ____________________ QUANTITY ____________________

PRICE ____________________ TERMS ____________________

START DATE ____________________ END DATE ____________________

NEW SUBSCRIPTION ____________________ RENEWA'L ____________________

ENTERED ON DATABASE ____________________

NOTES:

____

____

____

CHECKLIST:

_______ PAV

_______ DATABASE LOG SHEET

_______ XEROXES

_______ ENVELOPES

_______ LETTER

Title:

Publisher:

Wash. D.C. Rep: __________

Telephone: __________

No. of copies: ____

Copy	Sub. Per.	Price	Acct.#	Pur. O.#	Check#	Dt. Pd.

TITLE:

PUBLISHER	PRICE	SUB. PERIOD FROM	TO	DATE ORDERED	REQ. NO.	P. O. NO.

U.S. DEPARTMENT OF HOUSING AND URBAN DEVELOPMENT

HUD-738 (1-69) PERIODICAL ORDER RECORD 235568-P

SERIALS CHECK CARD

CLASS

TITLE

PUBLISHER

ADDRESS

PRICE ______________

FREQUENCY

A ______ SA ______ BA ______ OTH ______

VOLUME	NUMBER	YEAR	PUBLISHED	RECEIVED	REMARKS

TITLE

FREQUENCY

PUBLISHER
ADDRESS

BLANKET P.O.	
YEAR	NUMBER

YEAR OR VOLUME	NUMBER ORDERED	DATE RECEIVED	ORDER NUMBER	DATE	DEALER	PRICE

RECORD OF PERIODICALS ORDERED

TITLE

PUBLISHER

ADDRESS

SUBSCRIPTION			PRICE	REQUEST DATE	NO OF COPIES	PURCHASE ORDER	DATE RECEIVED	REMARKS
YEAR	FROM	TO						

SERIAL EVALUATION

Evaluator:_______ Date:________

Call No.____________________________ ISSN:___________

Serial Title:____

____

Date of Last Issue:_________
Journal__________
Newsletter__________
Monographic Series_____________

Major Emphasis:

Subject:____

Geographic Orientation:___________________________

Contents:

Articles: Case Studies:______________________
How to Information:________________
Research Emphasis:________________
Newsy:______________________________

Book Reviews:	Yes______	No______
Bibliographies:	Yes______	No______
Future Conferences, Courses, etc.	Yes______	No______
Key Contacts:	Yes______	No______

Evaluation:

Excellent______
Good___________
Fair___________

Recommend for Core List:	Yes______	No______
Route to	Yes______	No______

Comments:____

____

____

____

Attach AGRICOLA print out here:

SUBSCRIPTION RENEWALS

TO: ______________________________ DATE: ______________

You are on the distribution list
for the following journal: ______________________________

The journal is now due for renewal.
The price of the subscription is $_____ per year.
Please evaluate how valuable the journal
information is to your work or professional
development and recommend whether the journal
should be renewed.

☐ RENEW

☐ DO NOT RENEW

COMMENTS: ______________________________
____
____

PLEASE RETURN TO LIBRARY

SUBSCRIPTION RENEWAL FORM

To:	
From:	Date:

Attached is the annual subscription renewal list for your department. Disregard those titles which are marked-off as they are not up for renewal at this time.

In order for the Library to renew these subscriptions, we need for you to do the following:

1. Indicate beside each title if you wish to renew or to cancel the subscription.

2. Indicate the project number to which each subscription renewal is to be charged.

3. Return the approved form to the Library (mailstop) by ________________, as we cannot guarantee continuity of your subscription if the forms are not returned promptly.

If you have any questions, please call me at extension .

Departmental Approval:	Project Number:
Notes:	

CLAIM TO SUBSCRIPTION AGENT

* CLAIM NOTICE * * CLAIM NOTICE *
* CLAIM NOTICE * * CLAIM NOTICE *

09/14/89

CLAIM ISSUED TO: HARRASS ON ORDER NO.:

TITLE: WISSENSCHAFTLICHE BEITRAGE DER MARTIN-LUTHER-UNIVERSITAT HALLE-WITTENBERG
PUB: MARTIN-LUTHER-UNIVERSITAT
CITY: HALLE
ISSN: 0440-1298 CODEN: MLWBBJ
ADDRESS: VEB KONGRESS-UND WERBEDRUCK, 9273 OBERLUNGWITZ, EAST GERMANY 111 12 12

WE HAVE NOT RECEIVED THE FOLLOWING ISSUE(S) ON THE ABOVE ORDER:

EXPLORATIVE UND KONFIRMATORISCHE DATENANALYSE

THIS CLAIM IS FOR COPY NO. 01 OF 1 COPIES ORDERED. PREVIOUS CLAIMS SENT:

PLEASE SUPPLY OR ADVISE. PLEASE CHECK THE APPROPRIATE RESPONSE(S):

( ) ISSUE ENCLOSED

( ) REPLACEMENT SENT. DATE SENT: ______________________

( ) PUBLICATION DELAYED. EXPECTED PUBLICATION DATE: ________

( ) ISSUE COMBINED WITH ______________________________

( ) FREQUENCY HAS CHANGED. NEW FREQUENCY: ______________

( ) TITLE HAS CHANGED. NEW TITLE IS: ____________________

( ) NEVER PUBLISHED.

( ) TITLE HAS CEASED.
VOL./ISSUE NO. AND DATE OF LAST ISSUE: ______________

( ) OUT OF PRINT.

( ) NOT YET PUBLISHED. EXPECTED PUBLICATION DATE: ________

( ) OTHER: ______________________________________

PLEASE RETURN A COPY OF THIS NOTICE WITH YOUR RESPONSE. THANK YOU FOR YOUR ATTENTION TO THIS MATTER.

SERIAL RECORDS SECTION-CLAIMS

PHONE:

TELEX:
FAX:

CLAIM TO PUBLISHER

* CLAIM NOTICE *

* CLAIM NOTICE *

09/25/89

VISUAL INFORMATION SYSTEMS
ONE HARMON PLAZA
SECAUCUS NJ 07094

DEAR SIR,

PLEASE SUPPLY ISSUES NOT RECEIVED ON OUR STANDING ORDER FOR THE TITLE LISTED BELOW:

TITLE: VIDEO JOURNAL OF DERMATOLOGY
PUB: VISUAL INFORMATION SYSTEMS
CITY: SECAUCUS NJ (ISSN:)

VOL 2 NO 1 (1987) AND ALL LATER. PLEASE SEND US AN INVOICE IF PREPAYMENT IS REQUIRED. THANKS!

THIS CLAIM IS FOR COPY 01 OF 1 COPIES ORDERED. PREVIOUS CLAIMS SENT:

COULD YOU PLEASE SUPPLY THESE MISSING ISSUE(S), OR PROVIDE ANY INFORMATION ABOUT THEM?

PLEASE CHECK THE APPROPRIATE RESPONSE(S):

( ) ISSUE ENCLOSED

( ) REPLACEMENT SENT. DATE SENT: ______________________

( ) PUBLICATION DELAYED. EXPECTED PUBLICATION DATE: ________

( ) ISSUE COMBINED WITH ______________________________

( ) FREQUENCY HAS CHANGED. NEW FREQUENCY: ______________

( ) TITLE HAS CHANGED. NEW TITLE IS: __________________

( ) NEVER PUBLISHED.

( ) TITLE HAS CEASED. VOL./ISSUE NO. AND DATE OF LAST ISSUE: ______________

( ) OUT OF PRINT.

( ) NOT YET PUBLISHED. EXPECTED PUBLICATION DATE: ________

( ) OTHER: ____

PLEASE RETURN A COPY OF THIS NOTICE WITH YOUR RESPONSE. THANK YOU FOR YOUR ATTENTION TO THIS MATTER.

HEAD, SERIAL RECORDS SECTION

PHONE:

TELEX:
FAX:

Date____________________________

To:____________________________________

____

____

____

To Whom It May Concern:

Our current serial records indicate that the publication which has been received from your organization is a defective copy entitled:

____

____

Defective issue____

This is not a purchase order. Do not send invoices or set up subscriptions, but supply information below:

__________We will supply the issue(s).

__________Issue(s) are out-of-print and therefore unavailable.

__________Issue(s) will not be available because,______________________________

____

Please return this completed form and publication to:

Attention:______________________

Thank you for your attention to this matter. Your cooperation is appreciated.

Side 1

We are very grateful for the materials which you have been kind enough to send us on a gift or exchange basis. In checking our files, we find that the issues listed below have not been received. We shall appreciate it very much if these can be sent to us at this time. If the material listed is not available, please explain using the appropriate spaces on the back of this form. Thank you for a prompt reply.

Materials sent: ______________________ Date: __________

Out of print: ______________________

Not yet published: ______________________ Expected: __________

Remarks: ______________________

____

____

____

____

Side 2

CLAIM REQUEST FORM

TO: Acquisitions Department DATE: ____________________

FROM: ______________________________

☐ D.O./Mailing list ☐ D.O./S.O. ☐ FAXON ☐ UNIVERSITY MICROFILMS ☐ NTIS ☐ GPO(Subscription) ☐ BERNAN ☐ MEMBERSHIP	USE LITERATURE REQUEST FOR THESE CATEGORIES: D.O. D.O./Exchange D.O./GPO
REMARKS:	DATE CLAIMED:
MISSING ISSUE:	DATE RECEIVED:

KARDEX
ENTRY:

PERIODICAL CLAIM

Date ____________________

Title ____________________

____

Periodicals Department
Main Library
XXXX Corporation
5000 K Street, N.W.
Washington, D.C. 20000
(202) 444-7777

We have not received the issue(s) listed below.
Please supply or report if unavailable. Thank you.

Address on subscription, if different from above:

XXXX Corporation
General Library
Washington, D.C. 20000

INQUIRY

According to our records, we have not received the periodical issue(s) listed below. We are on your complimentary mailing list for this title and would appreciate receiving the missing issues.

IF THERE IS A CHARGE FOR THE PUBLICATION(S), DO NOT SEND WITHOUT FURTHER AUTHORIZATION.

Thank you for your courtesy in this matter.

Title	Missing issues

PLEASE RETURN ONE COPY OF
THIS FORM WITH THE ITEM(S) TO:

XXXX Corporation
General Library -- Serials Desk
5000 K Street, N.W.
Washington, D.C. 20000

(202) 777-4444

XXXX Corporation
General Library
Washington, D.C. 20000

CLAIM

According to our records, we have not received the periodical issue(s) listed below. We would appreciate being supplied with these issues.

This is a paid subscription. IF THERE IS A CHARGE FOR REPLACEMENTS, DO NOT SEND WITHOUT FURTHER AUTHORIZATION.

Thank you for your courtesy in this matter.

Title	Missing issues

PLEASE RETURN ONE COPY OF
THIS FORM WITH THE ITEM(S) TO:

XXXX Corporation
General Library -- Serials Desk
5000 K Street, N.W.
Washington, D.C. 20000

(202) 777-4444

Industry Association
Member Information Center
Washington, D.C. 20000

Good day,

Our library has been receiving your publication:

[Annual reports, editions, factbooks, etc.]

The latest edition we have is:

If you have issued anything later, we would be most grateful to receive a copy for our collection.

Sincerely,

Industry Association
Member Information Center
Suite 1000
5000 K Street, N.W.
Washington, D.C. 20000

(202) 777-4444

Industry Association
Member Information Center
Washington, D.C. 20000

Good day,

In checking our periodical records for your publication:

we find that we have not received the following issues on our subscription:

We would appreciate being supplied with these back issues.

Sincerely,

Industry Association
Member Information Center
Suite 1000
5000 K Street, N.W.
Washington, D.C. 20000

(202) 777-4444

LIBRARY ROUTING SURVEY
10/13/89

C , Katherine
Room

Listed below are the periodical titles routed to you. To remove your name from the routing of a particular journal, draw a line through the title. If you want additional titles routed to you, add the title to this list. Thank you.

GEORGETOWN JOURNAL OF LEGAL ETHICS

Routing Slips printed on perforated stock

Journal: AMERICAN BANKER

Copy: 3

____ Room PA-2030
____ Larry Room PA-3004
____ Harry Room PA-3017

Journal: AMERICAN BANKER

Copy: 8

____ Edward Room F-409
____ John Room G-4040
____ Elizabeth Room 6098
____ Credit Union Room 7114

Journal: WALL STREET JOURNAL

Copy: 2

____ Casey Room G-4052
____ Stephen Room G-4062
____ Hector Room G-4057

Journal: WALL STREET JOURNAL

Copy: 3

____ Call Reports Analysis Unit Room F-551

Routing slip generated by on-line check-in system

XXX Corporation
Central Library
Washington, D.C.

Serials routing

Please cross off your name, add date, and
forward as soon as possible.

National Journal
Vol. 22, No. 2, Jan. 13, 1990

1/12/90

Name	Department	Date
______________________	__________	__/__/__
______________________	__________	__/__/__
______________________	__________	__/__/__
______________________	__________	__/__/__

Last person, please return to Central Library, Room 100.

Do not remove this slip.

	Date
TITLE:	

1. Do not hold.
2. Send to next person within 2 days of receipt.
3. Photocopy any material you need longer than 2 days.
4. Cross out your name, initial, and write date out.
5. If you are out of town, have your name re-written at bottom of list.

TO:	Dept.	Initials	Date Out
1.			
2.			
3.			
4.			
5.			
6.			
7.			
8.			
9.			
10.			
11.			
12.			
13.			
LIBRARY			

LIBRARY ROUTING SLIP
PERIODICALS

1. ______________________________

2. ______________________________

3. ______________________________

4. ______________________________

5. ______________________________

6. ______________________________

7. ______________________________

8. ______________________________

9. ____________LIBRARY____________

Please pass on as quickly as possible.

Cross out your name and put in out-going mail when finished.

LIBRARY

JOURNAL______________________________

VOL./NO.______________________________

PITMAN______________________________
GOLDSTEIN______________________________
WALKUP______________________________
JOHNSON______________________________
ORR______________________________
SHAMPAN______________________________
LIBRARY______________________________

COMMENTS:

GENERAL LIBRARY STATISTICS

Statistics of library usage and work performed are kept by the various functional divisions of the library. Most managers will also compile these statistics into monthly and yearly reports to provide an overview of the library's services and accomplishments.

These summary reports may include all of the categories on the library's weekly reports or may highlight only the most important figures. The latter is particularly useful if the summary report is passed on to higher levels of management in the organization.

A collection of accurately completed monthly statistics forms can provide the library manager with a great deal of information about the library's operations, which should be used in planning the budget and work for the following year. An examination of a year's forms will tell the manager when the peak work periods are for the library as a whole and for individual departments or work areas. This information can, in turn, suggest adjustment in staffing or procedures.

The monthly form can be converted into a yearly form, giving the library manager the total activity for the year in each area. The yearly forms can be compared in much the same way as the monthly ones. Thereby, providing concrete documentation of the library's work over a longer period of time. If increases in library use, acquisitions, or circulation are evident in each succeeding year's statistics, library managers can use this documentation to advantage in their annual budget presentations to higher levels of management. Graphs and charts are easily compiled when the data are clearly arrayed on a well-designed form.

Public Services Profile **Month:**

Part A. Information Transactions

		Staff	Non-staff
I.	Reference Activities		
	A. Instruct./Ready Ref.		
	B. Search, 15 min. 1 hr.		
	C. Extended Search, 1 hr.+		
	1. No charge		
	2. User fee		
	Grand Total		
II.	Directional (public areas)		

III.	Automated Searches		
	A. Online		
	1. No charge		
	2. User fee		
	B. CD-ROM & Laser Disc		
	C. OCLC		
	Grand Total		

		No. Inq.	No. Dist.
IV.	Publications		
	A. Specific title requests		
	B. Reference request		
	C. Outreach purposes		
	1. Subject oriented		
	2. All other		
	Grand Total		

Part B. Outreach and Training

		No. Events	No. Reached
V.	Outreach Activities		
	A. External contacts & events		
	1. Ext. meetings/project startup		
	2. Exhibits/presentations		
	3. Tours/orientation/training		
	4. Unsolicited mailings		
	Grand Total		
	B. Technology Demonstrations		
	1. Online Systems		
	2. Bulletin Board		
	3. CD-ROM		
	4. Expert Systems		
	Grand Total		
	C. Training Programs		
	1. Library orientation		
	2. Research technique workshop		
	3. Other		
	Grand Total		
	D. Tour Program		
	1. Domestic visitors		
	2. Foreign visitors		
	Grand Total		

Name________________________

Month/Year________________________

REFERENCE TRANSACTIONS

Monthly Statistics
by User Category

							TOTAL
	Faculty	Fellow	Resident	Student	Staff	Alumni	
Basic Science							
Dentistry							
Medicine							
Nursing							
University							
TOTAL							

Name________________________

Month/Year________________________

Research and Extended Research

Monthly Statistics
by User Category

		Faculty	Fellow	Resident	Student	Staff	Alumni	SUBTOTAL	TOTAL
Basic Science	Catalog Check								
	Research								
	Extended Research								
Dentistry	Catalog Check								
	Research								
	Extended Research								
Medicine	Catalog Check								
	Research								
	Extended Research								
Nursing	Catalog Check								
	Research								
	Extended Research								
University	Catalog Check								
	Research								
	Extended Research								
TOTAL	Catalog Check								
	Research								
	Extended Research								

Non-University	Catalog Check		
	Research		
	Extended Research		

GRAND TOTAL	Catalog Check		
	Research		
	Extended Research		

RETROSPECTIVE SEARCH SERVICES

________(Month/Year)

	---LAST YEAR---		---THIS YEAR---	
	Same Month	Cumulated 1 July--	Current Month	Cumulated 1 July--
I. Requests completed				
II. Source of requests				
BASIC SCIENCE				
Faculty				
Staff				
Students				
Residents				
Fellows				
SUBTOTAL				
DENTISTRY				
Faculty				
Staff				
Students				
Residents				
Fellows				
SUBTOTAL				
MEDICINE				
Faculty				
Staff				
Students				
Residents				
Fellows				
Allied Health				
SUBTOTAL				
NURSING				
Faculty				
Staff				
Students				
SUBTOTAL				
COLLEGE				
Faculty				
Staff				
Students				
SUBTOTAL				
OTHERS				

MONTHLY LIBRARY REPORT

_______________, 19___

I. STATISTICS

A. Circulation

1. Circulating books ________
2. Reference books ________
3. Serials ________
4. Congressional documents ________
5. Microforms ________
6. GAO reports ________
7. CBO reports ________
8. ILL (external) ________

Total ________

B. Interlibrary loan

1. Requests submitted ________
2. Requests satisfied ________

C. Acquisitions

1. Circulating books ________
2. Reference books ________
3. Bound journals ________
4. Congressional documents ________
5. GAO reports ________
6. CBO reports ________
7. Microforms ________

Total ________

D. Serials (Detail in Section II)

1. Subscriptions initiated ________
2. Subscriptions cancelled ________

E. Photocopies

1. Staff ________
2. External ________

Total ________

II. SERIAL TITLES

Initiated	Cancelled

III. PERSONNEL

IV. PROJECTS

STATISTICS FOR THE WEEK OF ______________ 19___

CIRCULATION					
Books & Periodicals Charged Out					
Books Out for Photocopying					
Books Borrowed from Outside					
Books Loaned to Outside					
CATALOGING					
New Titles Cataloged					
Added Copies					
Books Processed					
Continuations--Added Volumes					
Reclassifications					
Withdrawn or Lost					
ACQUISITIONS					
Books Ordered					
Periodicals Ordered					
TELEPHONE					
Calls Into Library					
Calls Out of Library					
REFERENCE					
In-House Publications					
Ready Reference					
Extended Search					
Photocopying Service					
Publications Orders					
Messenger Dispatch					
Referral					

LIBRARY STATISTICS

Name

Date		TOTAL
REFERENCE		
READERS IN THE LIBRARY		
CIRCULATION		
Books and Pamphlets		
Periodicals routed		
Borrowed from Outside Sources		
	TOTAL	
BIBLIOGRAPHY		
HPR (Items in issue)		
Other bibliographies - Items		
	TOTAL	
ORDER		
Purchase		
Free		
ACQUISITIONS		
Books and Pamphlets		
Serials		
	TOTAL	
CATALOGING		
Publications cataloged		
Cards typed		
Cards filed		
Publications processed		
MAINTENANCE		
Overdue notices and telephone recalls		
Filing and Shelving		
Cards filed (Other than cataloging)		
Typing (If not counted above)		
Discards		

PROGRAM INFORMATION CENTER		
Telephone Calls		
Visitors		
Publications Distributed		

LIBRARY REFERENCE STATISTICS
For the month ____________

I. Interlibrary Loan

Number of Loans Borrowed (non-owned items) ____________

Number of Loans Borrowed (owned, but missing) ____________

Total Loans Borrowed ____________

Average Cost per Loan ____________

Total Cost of All Loans for the Month ____________

Number of Loans Loaned ____________

II. Computerized Information Retrieval

Database	Total Cost	Total Time HH/MM/SS	Total # Searches
Aviation Aerospace Online			
Berry Best			
Datatimes			
Dialog			
Dow Jones			
Dun & Bradstreet			
Legislate			
LEXIS/NEXIS			
Newsnet			
Nora			
OCLC			
Statenet			
Vutext			
Washington Alert			
Westlaw			

III. Reference Requests

Number of Reference Requests Completed ____________
Number of Information Requests Completed ____________

Week ending________

LIBRARY STATISTICS

Inquiries received

Staff ________________ | Member ________________

Letter ________________ | Non-member________________

Phone ________________ | Library________________

In person________________

Form letters sent________________ Business letters written________

Inquiry letters written________________

Materials acquired________________

Materials cataloged

Fully cataloged ________________

Classified only________________

Materials requested

Books and reports ________________

Periodical articles________________

Requested by phone________________

Periodicals looked at for indexing and acquisition________________

Special indexes and periodicals looked at for acquisition________________

Materials circulated________________

Interlibrary loan

Items requested by us________________

Items requested of us________________

Items sent by us________________

P&P written________________

Special projects

Acquisitions and Inter-Library Loan

______________, 19__

A. <u>Acquisitions</u>
(Number of items ordered in each category)

Purchase (except GPO, NTIS)	_____
GPO	_____
NTIS	_____
Free	_____
Review copies requested	_____
Rev. cop. rec'd unsolicited	_____
Rev. cop. paid	_____

B. <u>Inter-Library Loan</u>

Items borrowed	_____
Photocopies received	_____
Items lent	_____
Photocopies provided	_____
Requested from us, not owned	_____
Requested from us, in use	_____
Requested from us, missing	_____
Requested by staff, unlocated	_____

Monthly Library Report

__________, 19___

New materials acquired for Library

Books:
    Purchased:
    Gifts:
Documents:
Periodical subscriptions:
    Agents:
    Direct:
    GPO:

Materials cataloged

Books:
Documents:
Periodicals:

Materials processed

Books:
Documents:
Periodicals:

Materials withdrawn:

Bindery

Volumes sent:
Volumes received:

Materials used/circulated

Books:
Documents:
Periodicals:
Folders/technical files:
Overdue contacts:
Inter-library loans:
    Borrowed:
    Lent:

Reference

	Rec'd.	Compl.	Pending
Requests from headquarters:			
Requests from branches:			
Requests from public:			

Number of users:

Photocopies made:

Overtime Hours:

COLLECTION MANAGEMENT STATISTICS

Branch: ______________________ Month: ______________________

MONOGRAPHIC VOLUMES* RECEIVED

Include monographs, trade catalogs, monographic series* cataloged as separates, transfers* from other branches, duplicates, and bar-coded surrogates*. Exclude uncataloged materials, maps, and non-print materials.

When entering totals, use the figure 0 if there is no entry. Total:

BOUND SERIAL VOLUMES RECEIVED

Include physical volumes received from bindery, newly acquired bound serials or backruns, monographic series* cataloged as serials, transfers* from other branches, and annuals. Exclude uncataloged materials.

Total:

MICROFORM PIECES RECEIVED

Count microfilm reels and microfiche sheets. Include transfers* from other branches.

Total:

UNBOUND JOURNAL ISSUES RECEIVED

Total:

BOUND JOURNAL VOLUMES WITHDRAWN*

TRANSFERS TO ANOTHER BRANCH	WITHDRAWALS FROM THE SYSTEM
Total:	Total:

OVERTIME/COMPTIME REPORTING

NAME ____________________________

TYPE OF RECORDS ____________________________

NO. OF RECORDS KEYED ____________________________

DATE WORKED ____________________________

NO. HOURS & TIME ____________________________

OVERTIME/COMPTIME REPORTING

NAME ____________________________

TYPE OF RECORDS ____________________________

NO. OF RECORDS KEYED ____________________________

DATE WORKED ____________________________

NO. HOURS & TIME ____________________________

OVERTIME/COMPTIME REPORTING

NAME ____________________________

TYPE OF RECORDS ____________________________

NO. OF RECORDS KEYED ____________________________

DATE WORKED ____________________________

NO. HOURS & TIME ____________________________

OVERTIME/COMPTIME REPORTING

NAME ____________________________

TYPE OF RECORDS ____________________________

NO. OF RECORDS KEYED ____________________________

DATE WORKED ____________________________

NO. HOURS & TIME ____________________________

BUDGET

Accounting procedures vary widely from library to library, depending for the most part on the requirements of the parent organization. Some libraries control only their expenditures on books and periodicals, while supplies and overhead expenses are absorbed by the organization which they serve. Other libraries must account for every photocopy and telephone call and must work within a budget for each item.

The amount of detail required on budget forms will therefore depend on the number of categories for which the library must maintain records. Common to all, however, is the need to know how much has been spent at any point in time and how much money is left in various accounts. The forms which follow provide some examples of the ways in which libraries can keep track of individual expenditures and report totals.

SCHEDULE 1 - FUNDED ISSUES

LIBRARY BUDGET

	FY89	FY90	FY91
TRAVEL			
LEASES			
CONTRACTS			
SUPPLIES			
General			
Periodicals			
Books			
Non-Print Media			
Branch Library			
EQUIPMENT			
GRAND TOTAL			

BUDGET LINE ITEM REQUESTS

DIVISION	DESCRIPTION	PGM $

Status of Funds

FUND	PROGRAM $	EXPENDED	BALANCE	Notes
Grand Total				

Status of Funds

FUND	PROGRAM $	EXPENDED	BALANCE	Notes
Travel				
Contracts				
Supplies				
Equipment				
Materials				
Periodicals				
Books				
Non-Print				
Branch				
Grand Total				

PURCHASE REQUEST LOG

Purchase Instr Number	Date Forwarded	Division	Brief Description

DATE:

TO:

THRU:

FROM:

SUBJECT: Monthly Cuff Record Expenditures

MONTH:__________________

COST CODE	BUDGET AMOUNT	OBLIGATED THIS MONTH	OBLIGATED YEAR TO DATE	UNOBLIGATED BALANCE

VACANT POSITIONS:

OVERTIME:
Used this month__________________________________
Requirements next month____

Note: Use this standard format to conform with the Status of Funds Reports. Prepare and submit by the second Monday of each month.

TO : Chief Librarian. DATE:

FROM : Resource Librarian.

SUBJECT: Monthly Budget Report.

The current status of each of the library budgets is:

	UNOBLIGATED BALANCE	OBLIGATIONS AND EXPENDITURES	CURRENT UNOBLIGATED BALANCE	OBLIGATIONS AND EXPENDITURES TO DATE
SUPPLIES				
EQUIPMENT				
BOOKS				
GPO				
L.C.				
KRAMER 1)ORDERS 2)BILLS				

CUFF RECORD FOR USE BY A&F OFFICES

Budget Line Item Description ______________ Organization Code ______________
Account Symbol.............. ______________ Purpose Code..... ______________
Fund Code.................. ______________ Cost Code(s)..... ______________

	Document Date, FY___	Document Number	Cost Code	Transaction Description	Obligation Number	Obligations & (Deobligations)	Unobligated Balance
1							
2							
3							
4							
5							
6							
7							
8							
9							
10							
11							
12							
13							
14							

Account for ____________________

Address ____________________

____

DATE	FIRST READING	SECOND READING	NO. OF COPIES

TOT

x

AMT. O

MONTH ____________________ YEAR ________

	INCOME		EXPENDITURES	
DAY	PURPOSE	AMT.	PURPOSE	AMT.

DATE ______________________

NAME OF ACCOUNT TO BE CHARGED ______________________

ACCOUNT CODE NUMBER ______________________

FOR ACCOUNTING PURPOSES ONLY	
Charge	$______
Tax	______
Total	$______

COMPLETE APPLICABLE INFORMATION BELOW

/_/ TELEPHONE
(Including Telecopier)
Person called, made by
and telephone number

Indicate number of minutes:

/_/ 1-10; /_/ 10-15; /_/ 15-20;
/_/ 20-25; /_/ over 25

/_/ POSTAGE
Business replies or other
(Describe)

/_/ DELIVERIES
Messenger/Metro Messenger
From and to, date--if other
than above

/_/ TELEGRAMS AND CABLES
(Including Twx)
Place, sent by

/_/ OTHER
(Specify)

____
CHARGE PREPARED BY

ACQUISITIONS STATISTICS - MONTHLY TALLY OF ACQUISITIONS PAYMENTS

MONTH ____________

			TOTAL
PAYMENT VOUCHERS PREPARED	L.S. 04-0003-00		
	U.I. Staff other project #		
PETTY CASH REQUESTS	L.S. 04-0003-00		
	U.I. Staff other project #		
STATEMENTS			
REFUNDS			

1/77

Individual reports are maintained for each line item

ACQUISITIONS STATISTICS - MONTHLY AND CUMULATIVE REPORT

LINE 459 - EQUIPMENT RENTAL (including mailroom charges for xerox work*)

YEAR___________

MONTH	A. Expenditures Month Total	B. Expenditures Previous Total	Expenditures Cumulative Total (A+B)	CUMULATIVE REPORT FOR THE PERIOD___________		
				Invoices in Process	Encumbered (e)	TOTAL
JANUARY						
FEBRUARY						
MARCH						
APRIL						
MAY						
JUNE						
JULY						
AUGUST						
SEPTEMBER						
OCTOBER						
NOVEMBER						
DECEMBER						

e = estimated
* .03 per copy - .005 Line 463
.025 Line 459

1/77

ACQUISITIONS STATISTICS - MONTHLY AND CUMULATIVE REPORT

LINE 464 - LIBRARY MATERIALS (Publications)

PERIOD ________/________
MONTHS YEAR

CATEGORY	CURRENT MONTH				
	A. Expenditures	B. Invoices in Process	C. TOTAL (A+B)	D. Previous Expenditures	TOTAL TO DATE (C+D)
Monographs-D.O.					
Monographs-GPO					
Monographs-NTIS					
Memberships (incl.Brookings)					
Serials-D.O.					
Serials-FAXON					
Serials-GPO					
Serials-NTIS					
Serials-BERNAN					
Microfilms-current					
Microfilms-backfile					
Abstracts					
TOTAL					

RENEWALS PROCESSED FOR__________(job cost)

	Current Month	Previous Expenditures	TOTAL TO DATE
Serials-D.O.			
Serials-FAXON			
Memberships			

255 PAGE 1

1/77

ACQUISITIONS STATISTICS - CUMULATIVE REPORT INCLUDING ENCUMBRANCES

LINE 464 - LIBRARY MATERIALS (Publications)

______________ PERIOD COVERED

CATEGORY	1. Expenditures	2. Invoices in Process	3. Encumbrances	4. Previous Expenditures	5. TOTAL (all columns)
Monographs-D.O.					
Monographs-GPO					
Monographs-NTIS					
Memberships (incl.Brookings)					
Serials-D.O.					
Serials-FAXON					
Serials-GPO					
Serials-NTIS					
Serials-BERNAN					
Microfilms-current					
Microfilms-backfile					
Abstracts					
TOTAL					

RENEWALS PROCESSED FOR ____________ (job cost)

	Current Month	Previous Expenditures	TOTAL TO DATE
Serials-D.O.			
Serials-FAXON			
Memberships			

256 PAGE 2

NOTE: For Deposit Accounts: expenditures recorded reflect date of statement, not subscription period.

1/77

ACQUISITIONS STATISTICS - MONTHLY AND CUMULATIVE REPORT

MONTH________

LINE 463 - LIBRARY SUPPLIES, CATALOG CARD REPRODUCTION, AND MAILROOM XEROX CHARGES

				CUMULATIVE REPORT FOR THE PERIOD________		
	A. Expenditures Month Total	B. Expenditures Previous Total	Expenditures Cumulative Total (A+B)	Invoices in Process	Encumbered (e)	TOTAL
SUPPLIES						
CATALOG CARD REPRODUCTION						
MAILROOM XEROX CHARGES (estimated) *						

e = estimate

*.028 per copy - .005 Line 463
.023 Line 459

BOOKS AND MATERIALS BUDGET
TOTAL BUDGETED 250,600.00

MONTH	CUM%	DATE	SPENT/WEEK	SPENT/DATE	+/-TARGET	RETURNS	BALANCE
SEPT 20,048.00	(8%)	9/08	$5.00	5.00	20,043.00	$1.00	250.596.00
		9/15	$5.00	10.00	20,038.00	$2.00	250,593.00
		9/22		10.00	20,038.00		
		9/29		10.00	20,038.00		
OCT 35,084.00	(14%)	10/06		10.00	35,074.00		
		10/13		10.00	35,074.00		
		10/20		10.00	35,074.00		
		10/27		10.00	35,074.00		
NOV 55,132.00	(22%)	11/03		10.00	55,122.00		
		11/10		10.00	55,122.00		
		11/17		10.00	55,122.00		
		11/24		10.00	55.122.00		
DEC 117,782.00	(47%)	12/01		10.00	117,772.00		
		12/08		10.00	117,772.00		
		12/15		10.00	117,772.00		
		12/22		10.00	117,772.00		
		12/29		10.00	117,772.00		
JAN 132,818.00	(53%)	1/05		10.00	132,808.00		
		1/12		10.00	132,808.00		
		1/19		10.00	132,808.00		
		1/26		10.00	132,808.00		
FEB 152,866.00	(61%)	2/02		10.00	152,856.00		
		2/09		10.00	152,856.00		
		2/16		10.00	152,856.00		
		2/23		10.00	152,856.00		
MAR	(68%)	3/02		10.00	170,398.00		

10

OTHER ACTIVITIES AND OPERATIONS

Library operations have many facets. Several areas of activity were not covered in the preceding chapters and so are represented here.

Fee-based service is an area of increasing interest to special libraries. Model billing forms and worksheets appear on the following pages.

Many of our client patrons work in widely scattered corporate branches or are members of our national and international associations. But even when our client comes from the department just down the hall, we sometimes don't get much feedback on the quality of our services. Therefore, a few evaluation forms are included here to help us gauge our effectiveness.

Since special materials and services are a hallmark of special libraries, some aids for organizing a map collection and a few worksheets for indexing and abstracting are included to help get you started.

Many libraries must control access to some or all of their materials. Visitor registration documents are reproduced here as well. In addition to names and addresses, visitor logs can provide valuable information for outreach efforts and collection development. In turn, collection development activities relate to inventories, and some inventory guides and task sheets are part of this chapter, too.

10. Other Activities and Operations

A. Fee for Service

B. Service Evaluation

C. Map Collections

D. Indexing and Abstracting

E. Inventory

F. Visitor Registration

G. Miscellaneous

Fee for Service

PHOTOCOPYING

Job no. ....

Date:

Debit:

No. of copies ....

Account #:

Total Cost $ ....

Dept.:

Signature ....

Credit: Technical Library
Dept. 300

Account #

Signature ....

Fees and charges recorded on reverse of database search request form:

Search Analyst:________________ Formulation time: ________________ Date Completed:____________________

VENDOR	DATABASE(S)	CITATIONS		CONNECT		PAGES	
		ONLINE	OFFLINE	TIME	CHARGE	#	CHARGE
	TOTAL:						

METHOD OF PAYMENT:

CASH CHARGE INVOICE

Connect Time Charge $___________
Offline Citations ____________
Service Fees ____________
TOTAL $___________

Deposit received $___________
Date ____________
Initials ____________

Search authorization and charges information on reverse of database search request:

I authorize the Library to perform the search requested and agree to pay any staff or computer charges that are required. I understand that there is a $10.00 processing fee for each request. I further understand that I am obligated to pay these charges even if the search yields few or no citations or information.

The maximum that I am willing to pay is ________ and I understand that the librarian will make every effort to honor this maximum but cannot guarantee to do so.

Signed______________________________ Date________________

Bill to: (if different from address on reverse)

____

____

____

Time required	Begin	Stopped	Time Hour	Time Minute
Professional:	____	____	____	____
	____	____	____	____
	____	____	____	____
	____	Grand Total	____	____
Staff:	____	____	____	____
	____	____	____	____
	____	____	____	____
	____	Grand Total	____	____

Bibliography (search) supplied?

Yes ____

No ____

Date Received________________

Date Compiled________________

Attach summary of database costs, if any.

INFORMATION CENTER

Reference Service Fees
for Nonmembers

Photocopies	Bibliographies
$10 per article	$10 each

Biographical Searches

$15 per name

The Information Center requires prepayment with all orders.
We welcome personal checks and money orders; credit cards may be used for orders of $25 or over.

*Send to:

Shipping:

Name: ____________________

Attention: ____________________

Firm: ____________________

Address: ____________________

____

____

City State ZIP Code

*Please enter this account number on the face of your checks to speed up your order:

Side 2

ORDER FORM

Quantity	Title/Item	Price
	Total above	
	D.C. sales tax Add 6%	
	TOTAL AMOUNT	

PAYMENT METHOD

☐ Check enclosed (Make payable to the

☐ American Express ☐ Mastercard ☐ VISA ($25 minimum when using credit cards)

Credit Card Number ____________________

Expiration Date ____________________

Signature ____________________

Multi-part form combines invoice with request record and worksheet

Requestor ______________________

Firm name ______________________

Address ______________________

____

____

Phone ( ) ______________ S M SM NM GOV'T

Last 4 digits - Soc. Sec No. ______________________

Maximum Charge ______________________

Received: Date ____________ Time ________

Special handling:
Rush ________
FAX ________ Number ______________
FedExpress ____ Number ______________
Billing:
Bill me ______________________

[ ] Visa Card # ______________________

[ ] Mastercard # ______________________
Expiration Date ______________________

Charges:

395700	Research time ________ hrs.	$ ______
395600	Photocopy service ______ pgs. plus royalties $ ______	$ ______
395800	Book rental ________ titles	$ ______
395400	Banking Literature Index Search	$ ______
395500	Commercial database search ( )	$ ______
395100	FYI-Information Packet	$ ______
395000	Rush service	$ ______
395300	Fax _____ pgs.	$ ______
	Other ______________	$ ______
395200	Shipping & handling	$ ______
	Total	$ ______

REQUEST FOR ARTICLES: (Encourage mailing or faxing request)

1. JOURNAL ______________________ DATE: ______ PAGE: ______
   TITLE OF ARTICLE ______________________
2. JOURNAL ______________________ DATE: ______ PAGE: ______
   TITLE OF ARTICLE ______________________
3. JOURNAL ______________________ DATE: ______ PAGE: ______
   TITLE OF ARTICLE ______________________
4. JOURNAL ______________________ DATE: ______ PAGE: ______
   TITLE OF ARTICLE ______________________
5. JOURNAL ______________________ DATE: ______ PAGE: ______
   TITLE OF ARTICLE ______________________

REQUEST FOR BOOKS: (Encourage mailing or faxing request)

1. CALL # ______________ AUTHOR: ______________
   TITLE: ______________________
2. CALL # ______________ AUTHOR: ______________
   TITLE: ______________________
3. CALL # ______________ AUTHOR: ______________
   TITLE: ______________________
4. CALL # ______________ AUTHOR: ______________
   TITLE: ______________________
5. CALL # ______________ AUTHOR: ______________
   TITLE: ______________________

Multi-part form combines invoice with request record and worksheet

Requestor ____________________
Firm name ____________________
Address ____________________
____
____

Phone ( ) __________ S M SM NM GOV'T
Last 4 digits - Soc. Sec No. __________
Maximum Charge __________

Received: Date __________ Time __________
Special handling:
Rush __________
FAX __________ Number __________
FedExpress _____ Number __________
Billing:
Bill me __________
[ ] Visa Card # __________
[ ] Mastercard # __________
Expiration Date __________

Charges:

395700	Research time ______ hrs.	$
395600	Photocopy service ______ pgs.	$
395900	Royalties $______	$
395800	Book rental ______ titles	$
395400	Banking Literature Index Search	$
395500	Commercial database search ( )	$
395100	FYI-Information Packet	$
395000	Rush service	$
395300	Fax ______ pgs.	$
	Other ______	$
395200	Handling	$
	Total	$

Request:

Received by:

Reply:

Researcher __________ Cleared __________ Mailed __________ Time spent: _____ Hrs. 15 30 45 60 minutes

Photocopy / Fax Worksheet (circle one)

(Librarian fill out)

Your name___________________________Date__________
Client name____

Status (circle) S* M SM GOVT. NM ILL*

*If for staff or ILL no registration of copyright or royalty will be necessary.

(Photocopy staff fill out)

Photocopies

Total number of articles....................______

Total number of pages(excluding cover page)..______

@.25 /.50 (circle one)......$_____

Royalties........$_____

Total..........$_____

FAX

Total number of articles....................______

Total number of pages(excl. cover page transmittal letter and header)......______

$2 first page plus______pages at $1........$_____
$3 first page plus______pages at $1.50.....$_____

Royalties........$_____

Total..........$_____

Date completed________ Initials of photocopier______

Service Evaluation

Date______________________

YOUR ASSISTANCE, PLEASE

Once in a while we overlook something. If you've noticed some small thing that needs attention, won't you please take a moment to tell us about it?

It is our genuine wish to provide you with the excellence that we strive for and that you deserve; and we value your comments.

____

____

____

____

____

Name____

Telephone number______________________________

Department____________________________________

THANK YOU.

To: New Book Requestors

From: Library Acquisitions Program Office

QUESTIONNAIRE ON COLLECTION DEVELOPMENT

Enclosed is a newly acquired book you requested to see. To support our efforts to monitor the effectiveness of our program for acquiring new library books, we would appreciate it if you would take a moment to complete this brief questionnaire. Return it to the library.

Book Title: ______________________________

Please circle your answers

1. How would you rate the technical quality of this book?

1 Excellent; 2 Good; 3 Acceptable; 4 Poor; 5 Not a technical title

2. How would you rate the "readability" of this book, taking into consideration its style, format, organization, and illustration?

1 Excellent; 2 Good; 3 Acceptable; 4 Poor

3. For this book, did you read the entire book, or only a portion of interest to you?

1 75-100%; 2 50%-74%; 3 25%-49%; 4 Less than 25%

4. If you were disappointed in the book, what was the reason?

1 Content too technical

2 Content not technical enough

3 Title was misleading; subject not as expected

4 Poorly organized or written

5 Author not knowledgeable or errors in text

6 Did not have the specific information I was looking for.

7 Other ____________________

8 Was not disappointed

5. If you found the book valuable, why?

1 Answered a specific question I had.

2 Presented significant new material.

3 Good state-of-the-art review.

4 Book was not valuable.

5 Other____________________

6. On the whole, how do you feel that the firm library book collection is meeting your needs?

1 Very well; 2 Satisfactorily; 3 Poorly; 4 Cannot judge

7. Are the subject areas important to firm projects covered adequately in the Library's book collection?

1 Yes, reasonably good coverage on needed subjects.

2 No. State subject(s).

8. How many books would you estimate you have borrowed from the Library's collection in the last year?

1 Fewer than 10; 2 10-20; 3 21-30; 4 More than 30

9. If you could, would you purchase this particular book for your personal or project collection?

1 Yes 2 No

10. If you had to place a monetary value on time saved or knowledge gained in reading this book, the value would be:

1 Under $50; 2 $50-$250; 3 $251-$500; 4 $501-$1000; 5 Over $1000

11. Additional comments on library book collection:

Please indicate your department number: ______________

Return to

PLEASE RATE US ON OUR INFORMATION SERVICES: We want to serve you better. Do let us know how we did.

Did the information you received answer your question?
Yes____ No____ Please explain: ____________________

Would you request information from us again? Yes____ No____
Comments: ____________________

Would you recommend our service to a colleague? Yes____ No____
Comments: ____________________

How did you find out about our services? ____________________

Additional comments/suggestions ____________________

Would you like one of our staff members to contact you for follow-up services? Yes____

THANKS FOR YOUR HELP!!!!

NAME: ____________________

TITLE: ____________________

BANK/FIRM: ____________________

ADDRESS: ____________________

____

PHONE NUMBER: ____________________

To:

From: Extension:

Re your request of ____________ for ____________________.
date service provided

We want to serve you better. Please let us know how we did.

Did you find that your communication with the staff person working on your request was adequate? Yes______ No______
Please explain: ____________________

Did the information you received answer your question/meet your needs? Yes___ No___ Please explain: ____________________

____

Did you receive the service you requested in the agreed upon time frame? ____________________

Additional comments/suggestions: ____________________

____

____

____

THANK FOR YOUR HELP!!!

Please take a moment to complete this comment card.
Your input will help us monitor the quality of our resources and services.

Date ____________________ Are you a member ☐ Yes ☐ No

Was this your first contact with the Information Service? ☐ Yes ☐ No

What was the specific topic of your request? ____________________

Please rate the quality of resources used to answer your request.

☐ Excellent ☐ Good ☐ Fair ☐ Poor

Please rate the quality of service you received from the Information Service.

☐ Excellent ☐ Good ☐ Fair ☐ Poor

How long did it take to receive our response? _____ day(s)

Comments/Suggestions: ____________________

____

Optional: Name ____________________

Company ____________________

Phone ____________________

Thank you

CORPORATE INFORMATION SERVICES

Library Reference Request Evaluation

Your evaluation of this reference request will greatly assist us in maintaining high quality information services. Please complete this form and return it as soon as possible for our review.

NAME ____

DEPT/LOC________________________

REQUEST DATE_______________ DELIVERY DATE ________________

Research Subject____________________________________

____

Was the delivery time reasonable?

___YES ___NO

What percentage of the material was useful to you:

___100% ___75% ___50% ___25% or less

Did the material answer your question?

___YES ___NO

Comments____

____

____

Will the information from this reference request assist you in making a business decision or completing a sale?

___YES ___NO

Comments____

____

____

Fold this form in half, staple, and return to Corporate Library

Thank you for your cooperation.

Manager, Corporate Library

Services Evaluation

Name____ Date______________

Office______________________ Telephone______________ Mail Code______________

Thank you for using the Library! Please do us a favor and give us your evaluation of our services. We are here to serve you, and will use your comments to improve our services to meet your information needs. Your feedback matters to us! Please return the survey to the front desk.

Literature Searches	**Always**	**Usually**	**Rarely**	**Never**
The librarian is helpful in defining your research question.	☐	☐	☐	☐
The librarian is helpful in explaining what to expect from the search.	☐	☐	☐	☐
The response time meets your needs.	☐	☐	☐	☐
The search results are useful.	☐	☐	☐	☐
Reference Service				
The librarian is helpful in defining your research question.	☐	☐	☐	☐
The librarian is knowledgeable about your subject area.	☐	☐	☐	☐
The librarian is knowledgeable about relevant sources of information.	☐	☐	☐	☐
The librarian is cooperative and helpful.	☐	☐	☐	☐
Collection Retrieval				
The Library usually has the information you need.	☐	☐	☐	☐
The catalog is helpful in retrieving information.	☐	☐	☐	☐
Interlibrary Loan				
You obtain the document(s) requested:	☐	☐	☐	☐
The response time meets your needs	☐	☐	☐	☐

Do you feel the library services meet your needs? ☐ Yes ☐ No. Please explain. ______________

____

____

____

____

____

Additional Comments: or suggestions for improving Library services to make them more useful for you:

____

____

____

____

____

____

____

____

____

____

____

____

____

If we form a Library advisory group, would you be able to participate? ☐ Yes ☐ No

If yes, please make sure your name, mail code and telephone number are clearly listed at the beginning of the form.

EVALUATION FORM

ONLINE LITERATURE SEARCH

Name:____

MailCode:____

SearchTopic:____

____

Were your requirements met with the results of the search?

____ Yes ____ No

Did the response time meet your needs?

____ Yes ____ No

What is your overall evaluation of the search?

____Very Useful ____Useful ____ Not Useful

Comments:____

____

____

____

After filling out the form please leave it at the Reference Desk in the Library or drop it in interoffice mail.

Map Collections

DATE BORROWED ______ TYPE OF MATERIAL ______

NAME ______ DEPT ______ PHONE ______

PROJECT ______ BORROWER ______

PLEASE NOTIFY MAP COLLECTION (X   ) OF ALL TRANSFERS.

COUNTRY OR AREA ______ SCALE ______ DATE OF MAP ______

TITLE: ______

AUTHORITY: ______

PUBLISHER: ______

FILED

PHOTO COPY ☐ NO. OF COPIES ______ NO. OF SHEETS ______

COMMENTS: ______

REC'D FROM ______ DATE REC'D ______

COUNTRY OR AREA ______ SCALE ______ DATE TAKEN ______

TITLE: ______

SATELLITE & SENSOR: ______

SUPPLIER: ______

TRACING: ______

NGS ID#: ______

COMMENTS: ______

NO. OF COPIES ______ NO. OF SHEETS ______

FILED: ______

DATE REC'D ______

MAP ACQUISITIONS

NOTIS # ______________

OCLC # ______________ Date OCLC searched/downloaded ______________

New title __________ New edition __________ Added copy __________

Purchased __________ Dep/Exchge __________ Gift __________

Date received ______________

Source ____

____

____

____

Price ______________

NOTES ____

____

____

____

____

____

____

Input by ______________

MAP SELECTION FORM

________________ Source/Page #

________________ Prepared by/Date

________________ Approved by/Date

Ordered	received	title, scale, publisher, date, edition	#	cost per	total	publisher/ordering address

COMMENTS:

SEARCH SLIPS

Maps

IN PROCESS FILE (PC AREA)____________________

ON ORDER FILE____________________

COMPLETED ORDER FILE____________________

LS/2000____________________

OCLC____________________DATE__________

MAP SERIES
PROCESSING FILE____________________

MAP AUTHOR/TITLE CAT.____________________

MAP SHELFLIST____________________

LEDGER SHEETS____________________

LEGEND MAP SHELFLIST____________________

MAP CATALOGING BACKLOG____________________

MAP DRAWER____________________

PREORDER:

DATE______________SEARCHER______________

AFTER RECEIPT

DATE______________SEARCHER______________

COST____________________

MAP ACQUISITIONS TALLY SHEET

______________, 19__________

I. PURCHASED__________

Publisher__________

Vendor__________

Bookstore__________

Standing Order__________

II. MEMBERSHIP__________

III. DEPOSITORY__________

IV. EXCHANGE__________

V. STAFF GIFTS__________

VI. OTHER__________

SELECTIONS:

I. Librarian__________

II. Staff Sugg.__________

MAP SERIES PROCESSING MONTH OF:

SERIES SCALE	ED	SH	TL	ED	SH	TL	ED	SH	TL	ED	SH	TL	ED	SH	TL	TED	TSH	TTL
USGS																		
1:24,000																		
1:25,000																		
1:62,500																		
TOPO 1:100,000																		
SAT 1:100,000																		
TOPO 1:250,000																		
SAT 1:250,000																		
AK 1:25,000																		
AK 1:63,360																		
USGS/DMA																		
1:50,000																		
CANADA																		
PHOTO 1:50,000																		
MONO 1:50,000																		
TOPO 1:50,000																		
TOPO 1:250,000																		
LAND 1:250,000																		
TOPO 1:500,000																		
AUSTRALIA																		
1:100,000																		
TOPO 1:250,000																		
BATHY 1:250,000																		
NEW ZEALAND																		
1:25,000																		
1:50,000																		
1:63,360																		
1:250,000																		
PAIGH - THE AMERICAS																		
1:250,000																		
IMW																		
1:1,000,000																		
J.O.G.s																		
Topo 1:250,000																		
Aero 1:250,000																		
AERONAUTICAL																		
VFR 1:250,000																		
SAC 1:500,000																		
WAC 1:1,000,000																		
TPC 1:500,000																		
ONC 1:1,000,000																		
JNC 1:2,000,000																		
GNC 1:5,000,000																		
NAUTICAL																		
DMA																		
NOAA																		
BRIT. ADMIRAL																		
TOTAL FOR:																		

REPORT DOCUMENTATION PAGE

1. AGENCY USE ONLY *(Leave blank)*	2. REPORT DATE	3. REPORT TYPE AND DATES COVERED	
4. TITLE AND SUBTITLE			5. FUNDING NUMBERS
6. AUTHOR(S)			
7. PERFORMING ORGANIZATION NAME(S) AND ADDRESS(ES)			8. PERFORMING ORGANIZATION REPORT NUMBER
9. SPONSORING/MONITORING AGENCY NAME(S) AND ADDRESS(ES)			10. SPONSORING/MONITORING AGENCY REPORT NUMBER
11. SUPPLEMENTARY NOTES			
12a. DISTRIBUTION/AVAILABILITY STATEMENT			12b. DISTRIBUTION CODE
13. ABSTRACT *(Maximum 200 words)*			
14. SUBJECT TERMS			15. NUMBER OF PAGES
			16. PRICE CODE
17. SECURITY CLASSIFICATION OF REPORT	18. SECURITY CLASSIFICATION OF THIS PAGE	19. SECURITY CLASSIFICATION OF ABSTRACT	20. LIMITATION OF ABSTRACT

INDEXING WORKSHEET

NEW IND | IND/DATE | REV / DATE | TYPE

m s

DATE | ILL | CONT | BIB | LANG | FILE

CALL NUMBER

365

#a #b v. #c

NOTES
500

BIBLIOGRAPHY 504

@040
#a #d

LANGUAGES
041

#a #b

CATEGORY CODES
072

#a #a #a

PAGINATION
300

GEOGRAPHICAL TERMS (651)

CABVOC TERMS
650

UNCONTROLLED SUBJECT TERMS
653

AUTHORS 100

TITLE 242

TITLE 245

JOURNAL CODE__________/TITLE_____________________

VOLUME ______________

ISSUE/NUMBER______________

DATE ______________

TITLE____

____

____

AUTHOR(S)____________________________; ________________________________

PAGE: LEAD____________ END ___________ CONTINUED [ ]

SUBJECT 1) ___________ 2) ______________ 3)_____________ 4)__________

TITLE____

____

____

AUTHOR(S) ___________________________;_________________________________

PAGE: LEAD ____________ END_____________ CONTINUED [ ]

SUBJECT 1) ____________ 2)______________ 3) ___________ 4) ____________

TITLE____

____

____

AUTHOR(S)____________________________; ________________________________

PAGE: LEAD _____________ END_____________ CONTINUED [ ]

SUBJECT 1)_______________2)_______________3)_____________4)___________

Library Inventory Control Sheet

Task	Date Assigned	Date Done	Comments

STACKS - MASTER

FRONT OF LIBRARY

left	North	*right*	*left*	South	*right*
	33			34	
stair		*stair*	*stair*		*stair*
	31			32	
	29			30	
	27			28	
	25			26	
	23			24	
	21			22	
	19			20	
	17			18	
	15			16	
	13			14	
	11			12	
	9			10	
	7			8	
	5			6	
stair		*stair*	*stair*		*stair*
	3			4	
	1			2	

READING ROOM

SECTION # ____________ CALL #'s ____________________

LEFT SIDE - measure first

WALL | | | | | AISLE END
|---|---|---|---|---|
| | | | | |
| | count | | | |
| | | | | |
| | | | | |
| | | | | |

RIGHT SIDE - measure second

AISLE END | | | | | WALL
|---|---|---|---|---|
| | | | | |
| | count | | | |
| | | | | |
| | | | | |
| | | | | |

MEASURE THE NUMBER OF LINEAR INCHES OF ITEMS ON EACH SHELF

On count shelf, count the number of items in one linear foot

If call numbers change in mid-range, show where they change

GENERAL PURPOSE SHEET ITEMS ____________________

location ________________

MEASURE THE NUMBER OF LINEAR INCHES OF ITEMS ON EACH SHELF

GENERAL PURPOSE SHEET ITEMS ____________________

location ________________

sec 1	sec 2	sec 3	sec4	sec 5	sec 6	sec 7	sec 8

MEASURE THE NUMBER OF LINEAR INCHES OF ITEMS ON EACH SHELF

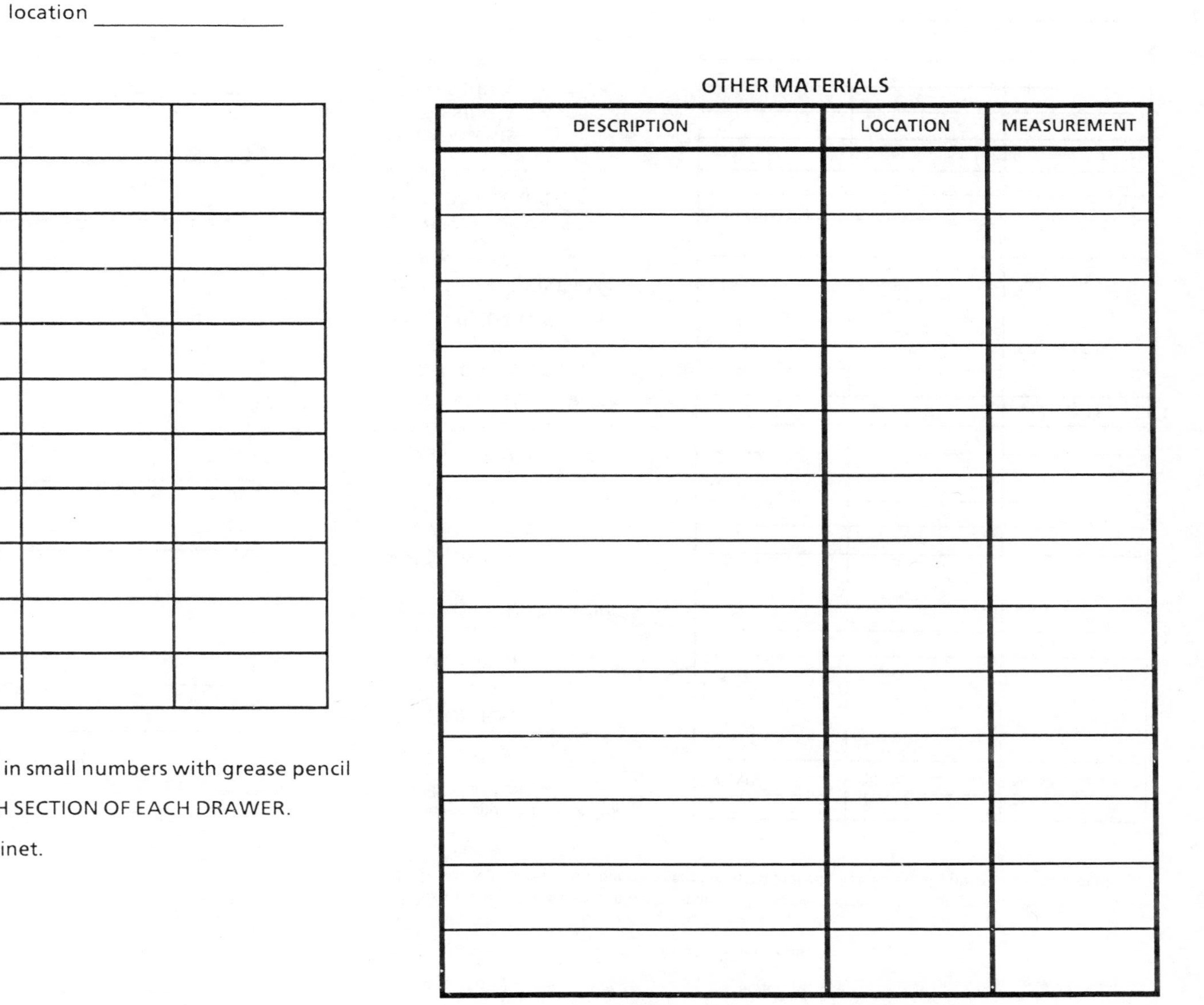

MICROFILM/ MICROFICHE CABINET # _____ location ________________
(circle film or fiche)

1					
2					
3					
4					
5					
6					
7					
8					
9					
10					
11					

write cabinet number on front right near the top in small numbers with grease pencil

MEASURE LINEAR INCHES OF MATERIALS IN EACH SECTION OF EACH DRAWER.

Cross out sections and drawers not present in cabinet.

OTHER MATERIALS

DESCRIPTION	LOCATION	MEASUREMENT

Side 1

___ Library does not own
___ Staff initials

DATE ______________

LOST MATERIAL FORM

(PLEASE PRINT CLEARLY)

YOUR NAME ______________________________

TELEPHONE NUMBER ____________ ROOM NUMBER ____________

JOURNAL

JOURNAL TITLE ______________________________

VOLUME ________ DATE ________ ISSUE ________

BOOK OR MONOGRAPH

AUTHOR / EDITOR ______________________________

BOOK TITLE ______________________________

CALL NUMBER ______________________________

PUBLISHER ______________________________

ITEM FOUND/PATRON NOTIFIED__________ STAFF INITIALS ________

DATE PLACED ON THE HOLD SHELF__________ DATE PICKED UP ________

Side 2

AREAS TO CHECK

FOR

MISSING MATERIALS

Staff Instructions: Please search for the material listed on the front of this page. Place a check mark in the boxes representing the places where you have looked. Please ask if you are unsure about how

(Choose the appropriate area for either books or journals,	DATE ____ NAME ____	DATE ____ NAME ____	DATE ____ NAME ____
FOR BOOKS:			
INNOVACQ TO CONFIRM DATA			
CIRCULATION			
3RD FLOOR BOOK STACKS			
NEW BOOK SHELVES			
SHELVING CARTS			
STUDY ROOMS			
CLASS RESERVES			
PROCESSING AREA			
REFERENCE AREA			
RARE BOOK CASES(IF APPLICABLE)			
FOR JOURNALS:			
INNOVACQ TO CONFIRM DATA			
BINDERY LIST			
CURRENT JOURNALS			
2ND FLOOR STACKS			
SHELVING CARTS			
STUDY ROOMS			
PROCESSING AREA			
SERIALS AREA			
DUPLICATE ROOM			

JOURNAL SEARCH REQUEST

Title:
Author:
Call Number:

Patron's Name:
Phone:
Address:

Deadline:

Entered in CA Function by:

BOOK SEARCH REQUEST

Title:
Author:
Call Number:

Patron's Name:
Phone:
Address:

Deadline:

Entered in CA Function by:

MATERIALS FOR WITHDRAWAL OR TRANSFER
(Circle One)

SERIAL OR MONOGRAPH
(Circle one)

CALL NO. ________________

ONLY ONE COPY FOR LOCATION

_____ (yes) _____ (no)

BARCODE MATCH?

_____ (yes) _____ (no)

VERIFIED OTHER COPIES BY BARCODE?

_____ (yes) _____ (no)

PRINTOUT OF MAR DISPLAY ENCLOSED?

_____ (yes) _____ (no)

SELECTOR'S INITIALS: ________________

COMMENTS: ________________

____

DATE: ________________

- -

TRANSFER FROM: ________________

TO: ________________

WITHDRAW AND FORWARD TO LC: ________________

REVIEW FOR SPECIAL COLL.: ________________

WITHDRAW AND FORWARD TO
Asst. Dir., Collections Mgmt. ________________

- -

CATALOG RECORDS USE ONLY

GRSN# ________________

SHELF LIST ________________

OCLC# ________________

VOLS. STATISTICS ________________

CONTACT BRANCH ________________

____

SPECIAL INSTRUCTIONS: ________________

____

DATE: ________________

SENT FOR CONTRACT
CATALOGING ________________

Visitor Registration

NAME *(Print Last, First, Middle)*

BUILDING	ROOM	TELEPHONE

TITLE

I/D	BRANCH/LAB

NAME OF SUPERVISOR OR LAB/BRANCH CHIEF	TELEPHONE

CHECK APPROPRIATE BLOCK(S)

- ☐ PERMANENT EMPLOYEE
- ☐ TEMPORARY EMPLOYEE
- ☐ STAFF FELLOW
- ☐ VISITING SCIENTIST*
- ☐ GUEST WORKER*
- ☐ CONSULTANT*
- ☐ POST DR. FELLOW*
- ☐ OTHER* *(Identify)* ____________

If you are other than a Permanent Employee, give date your appointment or assignment will terminate: ____________

*Please have sponsorship statement on reverse side completed.

Side 1

APPLICATION FOR LIBRARY ID CARD

I am herewith applying for Library Identification Card in order to avail myself of the Library Services.

I agree to abide by the prevailing policies and procedures adopted by the Library and to be responsible and liable for all material charged with this ID Card.

I am aware that the Library books and journals are Federal Government property.

I know that the Library maintains an electronic detection system to control the unauthorized removal of library materials and that if I do not have these materials properly charged, I will be subject to the revocation of my ID Card and/or legal prosecution.

____

SIGNATURE OF APPLICANT

STATEMENT OF SPONSORSHIP

I agree to be personally responsible for all material charged with the Library ID card issued to the applicant named below and that I will promptly advise you if expiration date should be changed.

APPLICANT'S NAME

EXPIRATION DATE

SPONSOR'S SIGNATURE AND TITLE

DATE

(Back)

LIBRARY USE ONLY Side 2

Side 1

APPLICATION FOR BORROWER'S CARD

Name ______________________ (last) ______________________ (first) Soc. Sec. No. ____________

Home Address ________________________________ Phone ____________

City ____________________ State ________ Zip Code ____________

Campus Address ________________________ (building/room) Ext. No. ____________

BORROWER'S RESPONSIBILITIES

"When I use this card, or permit its use, I acknowledge responsibility to:

- return all materials borrowed
- pay for fines accrued
- pay replacement costs of materials borrowed and not returned, or deemed non-returnable by the library."

Signature ________________________________ Date ____________

Side 2

THIS SIDE FOR OFFICE USE ONLY

Patron Status Code ____________

Barcode

Budget No. ____________

Validation ____/____/____

Expiration ____/____/____

☐ Regular ☐ Student

☐ Extension ☐ Other

Data Entered by Circ. Attendant: ________________________ (name)

Data Edited ____/____/____ by: ____________

Comment: ________________________________

____

____

Library Visitor Authorization

Print All Information Except Signature *Identification is Required*

VISITOR'S NAME	RANK	DATE(S) OF VISIT	CATEGORY I II III
ORGANIZATION & ADDRESS	TELEPHONE home duty		
	REFERRED BY (name, organization)		

INTEREST (subject area, scope, format, etc)

SECURITY CLEARANCE ☐ Unclassified Only ☐ Confidential ☐ Secret ☐ Top Secret

Certification (if applicable) __________

Security Manager Signature & Date __________

VISITOR SIGNATURE & DATE *I have read and understood the visitor rules*	APPROVING OFFICIAL SIGNATURE & DATE

DISTRIBUTION:

Part I - Approving Official *VISITOR RULES On Reverse Side*

BORROWER REGISTRATION FORM

Any patron who has a badge expiration date of less than three months from the date of this application will not be issued a library card.

To be filled out by the borrower (PLEASE PRINT)

Name ______________________________ ID no. (SSN) ____-____-____
last first middle

Home Institution ______________________________
Institution Department

Permanent Home Address ______________________________
(Address 1) Street

____
City State Zip

Address ______________________________
(Address 2) Department/Office

____
Building abbreviation and room number

Local phone number (   ) ______________________________
Area code

phone number ______________________________

I have read Information For Borrowers and agree to abide by regulations. I am responsible for all materials borrowed on my library card and will not allow anyone else to use it. I will report its loss immediately

____
Signed Date

LIBRARY AND RESEARCH CENTER

READER'S REGISTRATION FORM

Date ____________

Name ____
Last, First, Middle initial

Home address ______________________________________

Washington area address ___________________________

Name of affiliated institution or organization ____________

____

If a student, indicate degree sought and faculty member

directing research ________________________________

____

Principal materials desired _______________________

____

Purpose for which materials are requested ______________

____

____
(Signature of reader)

VISITOR REGISTER

DATE ______ Name ______ Company or Other Affiliation ______ Kind of Business You're In ______ Street ______ City and State ______ I am interested in ______ ______	DATE ______ Name ______ Company or Other Affiliation ______ Kind of Business You're In ______ Street ______ City and State ______ I am interested in ______ ______
DATE ______ Name ______ Company or Other Affiliation ______ Kind of Business You're In ______ Street ______ City and State ______ I am interested in ______ ______	DATE ______ Name ______ Company or Other Affiliation ______ Kind of Business You're In ______ Street ______ City and State ______ I am interested in ______ ______
DATE ______ Name ______ Company or Other Affiliation ______ Kind of Business You're In ______ Street ______ City and State ______ I am interested in ______ ______	DATE ______ Name ______ Company or Other Affiliation ______ Kind of Business You're In ______ Street ______ City and State ______ I am interested in ______ ______

REFERENCE/VISITOR LOG DATE________

@@@

VISITORS
STAFF________
MEMBER________
OUTSIDE________

REFERENCE/RESEARCH QUESTIONS
STAFF________ TELE________
MEMBR________ MAIL________
OUTSD________ WALKIN________

STAT______
HIST______
TECH______
MARKT______
ADMIN______
OTHER______

TOTALS
VISITORS______
INQUIRIES______
LOANS________

LOANS STAFF______ MEMBER______ OUTSIDE______
ILL LOANED______ BORROWED______

&&&&&&&&&&&&&&&&&&&&&&&&&&&&&&&&&&&&&&&&&&&&&&&&&&&&&&&&&&&&&&&&&&&&&&&&&&&&&&&&

NAME	/W	/T	/M/	DEPT/COMPANY INC. ADDRESS	/TELEPHONE NO./	REQUEST & ACTION INC. RESULTS

Vertical Files

MASTER CLASSIFICATION LIST UPDATES

MCL	DATE:
ATEX	NAME:
STAFF	

CHECK ONE:

	NEW FOLDER		SEE: REFERENCE		DELETE/DISCARD
	FOLDER SUBDIVIDED		SEE ALSO: REFERENCE		TO ARCHIVES
	CHANGE OF HEADING		FIRST CLIP		

PREVIOUS HEADING:	NEW HEADING:

STAFF SCHEDULE

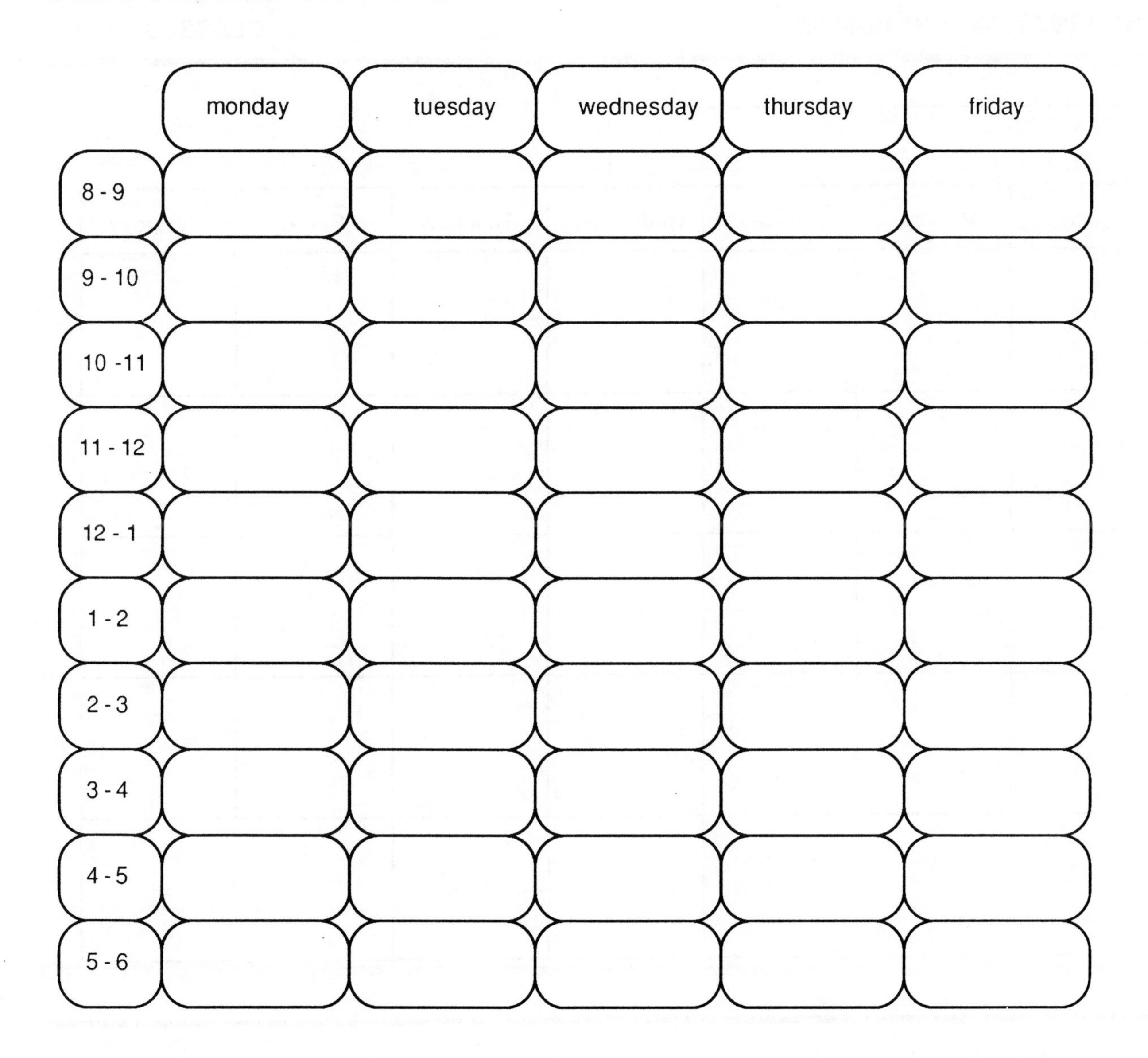

	monday	tuesday	wednesday	thursday	friday
8 - 9					
9 - 10					
10 -11					
11 - 12					
12 - 1					
1 - 2					
2 - 3					
3 - 4					
4 - 5					
5 - 6					

ON LEAVE:

Mon. -
Tues. -
Wed. -
Thurs. -
Fri. -

1989

CALENDAR OF COURSES

INFORMATION SEMINARS **CLASSES**

Sunday	Monday	Tuesday	Wednesday	Thursday	Friday	Saturday

LOCATION:

REGISTRATION:
ELIGIBILITY:

FEES:

(Over for Course Descriptions)

FAX TRANSMISSION

FAX NUMBER: (   )   VOICE PHONE: (   )

DATE: ____________________

TO: ____

____

ORGANIZATION: ____

____

FAX PHONE: ____________________

VOICE PHONE: ____________________

FROM: ____

SENDER PHONE: ____________________

TOTAL PAGES W/COVER: ____________________

ORIGINAL MAILED? ☐ YES ☐ NO

SPECIAL INSTRUCTIONS: ____

____

Completed: ______________________ Time: ______________________

FAX TRANSMISSION

DATE: ________________

TOTAL PAGES W/COVER: _______

TO: ____

ADDRESS: ____

____

FAX PHONE ____

VOICE PHONE ____

FROM: ____

ADDRESS:

FAX PHONE: (   )

VOICE PHONE: (   )

ORIGINAL MAILED: ________YES   ______NO

SPECIAL INSTRUCTIONS:

BIBLIOGRAPHY

I. Collections of Forms

Archival Forms Manual, compiled by the Society of American Archivists' Forms Manual Task Force. Chicago: The Society, 1982.

A compilation of "selected forms used in repositories representative of the entire archival spectrum." Includes samples from corporate, academic, government, historical society, and other archives. Forms are organized by function: appraisal and disposition; accessioning; arrangement and description; use (user registration, document requests); and specialized areas (conservation, loan agreements, loans, micro-reproduction, oral history, photoduplication, photographs, prospective donor information, solicitations, statistics compilation). Includes a bibliography of archival manuals.

Business Forms on File. New York: Facts on File, 1984.

Sample copies of forms and checklists. "Includes the forms most often requested from such agencies as the Internal Revenue Service, the Small Business Administration, Department of Labor, General Services Administration, and other government and quasi-government bodies." Also includes sample forms for general business and personal record keeping.

Futas, Elizabeth. *The Library Forms Illustrated Handbook.* New York: Neal-Schuman Publishers, Inc., 1984.

A collection of forms in use at public, academic, and government libraries. The reprinted forms are arranged in the following categories: technical services, public services, administrative services, audiovisual, and special collections. Each section begins with a discussion of forms use in that area of library operations for various types of libraries.

Kershner, Lois M. *Forms for Automated Library Systems: An Illustrated Guide for Selection, Design and Use.* New York: Neal-Schuman Publishers, Inc., 1988.

"Forms used with manual systems may be replaced by computer processing, but it is more likely that they will need to be modified and completely redesigned. New ones have to be created to accompany automated routines." A selection of sample forms in use at automated public and academic libraries, and forms designed by automated systems vendors. Forms are arranged in nine categories: acquisitions control; bibliographic database conversion and maintenance; patron registration and record maintenance; circulation control; patron requests; online reference searching; public use of microcomputers; automated systems operation; and administration and management reporting. Each section begins with a discussion of how the forms are incorporated into library systems. Not incorporated are forms that are self-contained within online systems as structured templates.

Toor, Ruth and Hilda K. Weisburg. *Complete Book of Forms for Managing the School Library Media Center.* West Nyack, NY: The Center for Applied Research, 1982.

A compilation of blank model forms ready to be photocopied and personalized by media centers. Forms are organized by the following functions: analyzing facilities and collection; developing personnel relationships and organizing clerical staff; circulation control; technical services; managing library programs (e.g. a book fair); working with teachers; working with the administration; correspondence; end-of-year activities; and professional growth and development. Each chapter begins with an explanation of that aspect of media center management. Includes as an appendix a directory of commercial suppliers of library forms.

Tweedy, Donald B., *"Principles of Forms Management," The Records & Retrieval Report 6(3)* March 1990 and 6(4) April 1990 (entire issues).

This two-part series reviews the basics of using printed forms in office records systems, featuring illustrations, checklists, and a glossary of terms. Part I focuses on forms management, while Part II discusses forms design and control. Suggestions for improving the efficiency of forms paperwork appear throughout.

Unruh, Betty and Martha Cornog, editors. *Forms and Responses: Volume One; Library/Acquisitions, Editorial and Production.* Philadelphia: National Federation of Abstracting and Information Services, 1986.

Sample forms and form letters contributed by abstracting and indexing services covering the library/acquisitions, editorial, and production functions of these services.

II. Periodical Literature

Fersko-Weiss, Henry, et al. "Forms Software Fills in the Blanks," *PC Magazine* 8(11) June 13, 1989, p. 139-206.

Describes the features and advantages of forms software packages. Accompanying articles discuss aspects of forms software and review packages available for personal computers.

Germann, Malcolm P., Elizabeth L. Nowak and Janet Stoeger Wilke, "Forms Design Simplifies Online Search Services Procedures," *Information Technology and Libraries* 6(4) December 1987, p. 313-316.

Chronicles the development of an online search form to meet the needs of the Wichita State University library. A single form was designed to combine information on search strategy, billing, and library statistics to replace the three separate forms previously used.

Howe, Nancy, "Documentation Takes Form," *Personnel Journal* 67(12) December 1988, p. 66-73.

Discusses the use of standard personnel forms along with ad hoc methods of documenting an employee's history. Recommends use of custom-made forms for certain personnel information needs.

Morton, Jim, "Designing Forms is a Snap with the Right Tools and a Little Know-how," *MacWorld* 5(2) February 1988, p. 291-304.

Overview of software packages available to create forms using the Apple MacIntosh personal computer. Includes advice on what to consider when designing a form.

Myers, Gibbs and Leslie A. Matthews, "Esthetics in Forms Design," *Journal of Systems Management* 35 (12) December 1984, p. 16-17.

Outlines the basic principles for achieving an attractive form design.

O'Malley, Christopher, "Forms Management Strategies," *Personal Computing* 13(8) August 1989, p. 74-82.

Discusses the advantages of using forms software to design and produce forms in-house rather than sending them out to be typeset. Surveys the capabilities of forms software packages on the market, and describes how specific firms are using them.

RASD Cooperative Reference Services Committee, "RASD's New Interlibrary Reference Request Form," *American Libraries* 16(5) May 1985, p. 298-299.

The Cooperative Reference Services Committee of the American Library Association's Reference and Adult Services Division developed a standard form for use in referring reference inquiries from one library system unable to answer the request, to another that can. The form, reprinted after an article discussing the need for and use of it, is a sort of interlibrary loan form for information rather than for documents.

Romei, Lura K. "Electronic Forms: Winning Against High Costs and Obsolescence," *Modern Office Technology* 34(4) April 1989, p. 42-48.

Overview of the advantages electronic forms software brings to businesses. Features related articles on the automated forms management program in operation at an insurance company.

III. Texts

Burgess, John H. *Human Factors in Forms Design.* Chicago: Nelson-Hall, 1984.

"This text provides criteria for assessing the appropriateness of a form for a specific application and the efficiency of its design from a human-factors point of view. Its purpose is to help government and business administrators reduce costs and improve productivity." Uses a systems analysis approach to evaluate a form's role in the organization's workflow, and a human engineering approach to evaluate its readability for the individual user. Includes critiques of some common forms in use by government and business, such as the Internal Revenue Service Form 1040.

Coates, Sarah and Edward I. Rudd, III. *How to Design Business Forms, 2nd edition.* Arlington, Virginia: International Business Forms Industries, Inc., 1982.

Concise, illustrated primer on forms analysis and design. Emphasis is on practical aspects of forms production, such as paper selection and preparation of copy for the printer. Includes brief bibliography and glossary of terms used in the forms business.

Jacobs, Marvin. *Forms design; the Basic Course—Plus!* Cleveland, Ohio: Marvin Jacobs, Formsman, Inc., 1980.

Includes chapters on the function of a form and on forms analysis. Emphasis is on design techniques.

Nygren, William V. *Business Forms Management.* New York: Amacom, 1980.

This basic text on forms management includes chapters on forms control, analysis, design, evaluation, and production. Appendices include job descriptions for forms administration personnel and a glossary of terms used in the field..

Schied, John P. *The Business Forms Handbook, 3rd edition.* Alexandria, Virginia: National Business Forms Association, 1984.

Standard reference text for business forms professionals includes a chapter on the development of the forms industry as well as a selective bibliography and glossary of terms.

United States. General Services Administration. National Archives and Records Service. *Forms Analysis and Design.* Washington: Government Printing Office, 1980.

This "handbook sets forth standards, guidelines, references and techniques for analyzing and designing effective forms." Includes chapters on designing for readability, filing and retrieving a form, and using typography. Includes as an appendix a checklist for forms analysis and design.

INDEX